The Complete Book of
TRAPPING

The Complete Book of
TRAPPING

BOB GILSVIK

Illustrations by David Gilsvik

CHILTON BOOK COMPANY

Radnor, Pennsylvania

Published in Radnor, Pa., by Chilton Book Company
and simultaneously in Don Mills, Ont., Canada,
by Thomas Nelson & Sons, Ltd.

Manufactured in the United States of America

Designed by Donald E. Cooke

LIBRARY OF CONGRESS CATALOGING IN PUBLICATION DATA

Gilsvik, Bob.
   The complete book of trapping.

   Includes index.
   1. Trapping.   I. Title.
SK283.G46   1976   639'.11   76-27660
ISBN 0-8019-6444-X

2 3 4 5 6 7 8 9 0   5 4 3 2 1 0 9 8 7 6

I am grateful to the Allcock Manufacturing Company for providing me with a great deal of information on how to use live traps. I am grateful as well to the Woodstream Corporation for their helpfulness.

Dedicated to NORMAN STRUNG
who made it all possible

CONTENTS

PART TWO: Pest Trapping

PART THREE: Live Trapping

INTRODUCTION

THE Complete Book of Trapping answers almost any question you may have about the subject. This manual is not only for those who trap for fur but for anyone who wants to know about traps and their use. The book is divided into three sections: Trapping for Fur, Pest Trapping, and Live Trapping. It explains how to trap mice under your kitchen sink and pocket gophers in your suburban garden, how to snare Canadian lynx, trap exotic marten and everything in between. It is an up-to-date guide, written for the modern trapper.

Trapping is older than recorded history. In North America, it has its roots deep in the practices of native Indians and early European settlers. As a livelihood it was second only to hunting in procuring essential food and clothing.

Trapping techniques and equipment are more refined today, but strict seasons and stringent regulations ensure a renewable harvest. Traps and those who set them have changed a lot over the years. Today few people rely on trapping as their sole source of income. People from all walks of life, Indians, farmers, school boys, rural mailmen, loggers, guides, game and fire wardens, even city dwellers are among those who go into the forest and field. In 1973 the State of Louisiana alone reported its 7,000 trappers took an annual fur harvest valued at more than $10.7 million. For some, the extra income is often a buffer against hardship. To others, it may be a means of paying for an education. Still others see trapping as a natural complement to their interest in hunting, fishing, backpacking, and camping. Trapping is a total outdoor experience that brings men and women into close contact with wildlife and the outdoors. Success demands a thorough knowledge of the animals one seeks, and it is often plain hard work. Yet, for many there is no greater form of recreation.

To the rancher or farmer, trapping can mean more than recreation or a financial return from furs. His very livelihood often depends on how well he uses traps to control depredation by wildlife.

Free-ranging livestock are particularly vulnerable to predators, especially during severe winter conditions when stock movement is hampered by snow. Claims for livestock destroyed by coyote amount to millions of dollars each year. In states such as Kansas, Oklahoma, Texas, Missouri, Colorado, and Wyoming, predation is often blamed for the decline in sheepherding in spite of high wool and lamb prices.

Trapping is also an important tool of wildlife research. Natural history studies frequently involve the trapping of individual animals so they can be examined, aged, sexed, weighed, tagged, then released unharmed. Retrapping these same animals later provides invaluable information on their movements and condition.

Controlling or limiting the spread of wildlife disease is essential to any wildlife management program. The more crowded animals are, the more likely is the development and transmission of disease. Of particular concern are diseases that can be transmitted to man. Rabies, tularemia, bubonic plague, Rocky Mountain Spotted Fever, and leptospirosis are among the most dangerous. Since 1959, two-thirds of the known rabies cases have been in wild animals.

Trapping affords the only logical means of controlling many wildlife populations and, if carried out in accordance with state and federal regulations, does not adversely affect the resource. In Ohio, for example, the Department of Natural Resources, Division of Wildlife, reports that muskrats comprise about 68% and raccoons about 27% of the pelts taken annually. Thus the two together make up about 95% of the harvest. Yet neither species is declining. In fact, the raccoon population has been increasing in recent years. If these heavily sought species are not threatened by regulated harvest, it is unlikely that other less sought after species are in danger because of trapping.

Yet antitrapping organizations who are, in most cases, antihunting as well, are actively seeking to ban the steel leg-hold trap (a misnomer since animals are invariably gripped above the toes on the foot) and trapping in general. The staff who head these groups are, unfortunately, often not professionally trained in wildlife management techniques. Many, in fact, know little or nothing about wildlife management. Their philosophy and opinions regarding wildlife are without foundation in fact and are often in total conflict with the proven techniques taught in college wildlife management courses across North America. Very seldom, if ever, are funds directed by such organizations to aid those wildlife programs supported by the hunter and trapper.

Responsible trappers are making every effort to realize the humane potential of the Conibear trap, named after its inventor Fred Conibear. This device is designed to kill quickly by breaking an animal's neck. To do so, however, the animal must enter the trap in exactly the right position, which does not always occur. Unavoidably, this trap is nonselective and can seriously harm or kill the unwanted animals it catches, including pets. The leg-hold trap, on the other hand, is designed to catch animals alive, restrain them, and leave to the trapper the decision to free or retain the captured animal.

Conibear traps have been found to be valuable in the taking of beaver, but they are also effective for such small game as muskrat, mink, and weasel in water sets and along animal runways. The large size Conibear, as used for beaver—which should be handled with extreme caution by the trapper because of its bone-crushing strength—is illegal for all but water trapping of beaver in some states. It is inadequate for the taking of shrewd land animals such as the fox, coyote, and wolf. The plain truth is, there is no practical substitute for the leg-holding trap, in spite of what others (who have never trapped) would have us believe.

Furbearing animals and predators have been taken in the steel trap for more than two hundred years, yet today they are still abundant except in areas where nature has taken its course and drastically reduced their numbers by sickness and death. While traps can and do destroy individual animals, nature itself can annihilate a species. Among the diseases which endanger wildlife populations are sarcoptic mange, a disease of red foxes caused by a mite living in the skin; and distemper, a viral disease that breaks out in raccoons and grey foxes when populations reach critical densities. A multitude of parasitic infections also continually threatens overly populated wildlife species. A well-managed harvesting program can remove excess animals, leaving those remaining healthier and more productive. Through the responsible use of the steel trap and the gun we can often maintain a better balance of predator and prey species than nature alone can provide.

In any group there are always a few whose irresponsible acts are highlighted to discredit the many who adhere to the law. As in any responsible group, trappers usually police themselves quite effectively. Many state trapping associations now offer training courses and insist upon a trapper's ethic, like the one below, as a personal and professional standard for their members.

A RESPONSIBLE TRAPPER MUST:

Obtain the landowner's permission before trapping on another's land.

Avoid setting traps in areas where domestic animals may get caught.

Set traps to kill quickly, utilizing water sets where possible.

Check traps regularly—preferably in the early morning.

Identify and record trap locations carefully and accurately.

Dispose of animal carcasses properly so as not to offend others.

Make an effort to concentrate trapping in areas where animals are overabundant for the supporting habitat.

Promptly report the presence of diseased animals to wildlife authorities.

Assist farmers and other landowners who are having problems with predators.

Support and help train new trappers.

Support strict enforcement of regulations including the reporting of all takes to state game agencies.

Part One

TRAPPING FOR FUR

Chapter
1
TRAPS and EQUIPMENT

A variety of steel leg-hold and body-grip traps, as well as self-locking snares, are available to the trapper. The two principal trap manufacturers are the Woodstream Corporation of Lititz, Pennsylvania, manufacturers of Victor, Oneida, and Newhouse traps; and Blake & Lamb of Cambridge, New York, manufacturers of Blake & Lamb traps. Leg-hold traps come in a variety of models including longspring, double longspring, underspring (jump trap), coil spring, and sure-grip or stop-loss in either the longspring or underspring model, in sizes from No. 0 for gopher, weasel, and barn rats to Nos. 4 and 4½ for wolf and beaver.

The use of either the longspring or underspring model trap is largely a matter of preference. Some prefer the underspring (jump trap) because it is compact, easy to conceal, and takes a high hold on the animal's foot. Others prefer the longspring for its tenacious gripping quality. All are adequate when used in correct sizes for the animals sought.

The body-grip or killer-type trap is best known in the Victor Conibear which comes in four sizes, 110, 120, 230 and 330. The Blake & Lamb No. 1 is another popular model. The body-grip trap is especially suited for the trapping of beaver and such water animals as mink and muskrat.

Snares, where legal, are a valuable asset to the trapper in wild terrain. The weight of carrying steel traps on foot, and the difficulty of keeping steel traps operating in deep snow, is a problem. Self-locking snares such as those manufactured by Raymond Thompson are effective for taking fox, coyote, wolf, bobcat, and lynx in thick cover and deep snow.

Generally, box traps are not used on the trapline. They are too bulky and costly to use in great numbers and are inadequate for the larger land

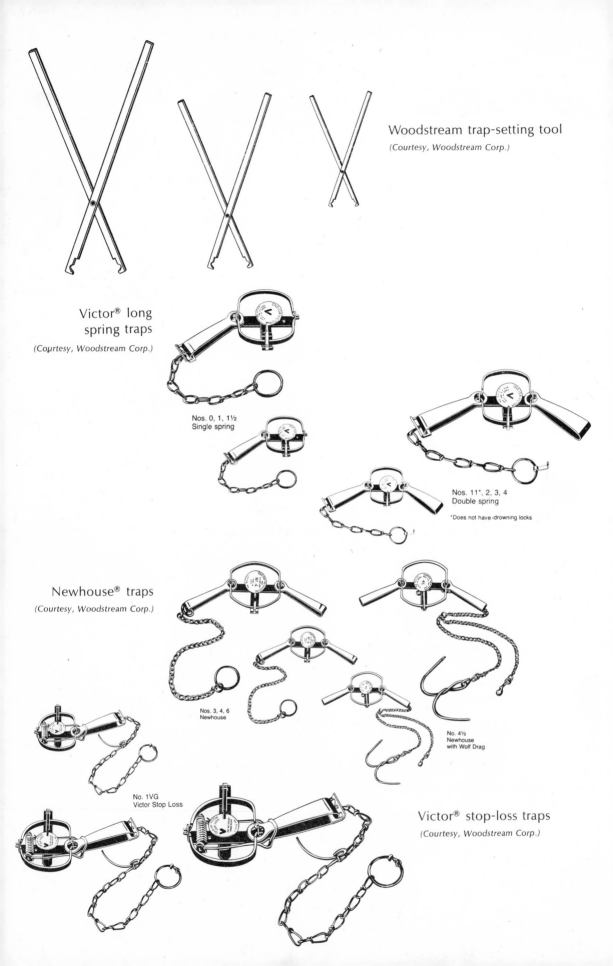

Woodstream trap-setting tool

(Courtesy, Woodstream Corp.)

Victor® long
spring traps

(Courtesy, Woodstream Corp.)

Nos. 0, 1, 1½
Single spring

Nos. 11*, 2, 3, 4
Double spring

*Does not have drowning locks

Newhouse® traps

(Courtesy, Woodstream Corp.)

Nos. 3, 4, 6
Newhouse

No. 4½
Newhouse
with Wolf Drag

No. 1VG
Victor Stop Loss

Victor® stop-loss traps

(Courtesy, Woodstream Corp.)

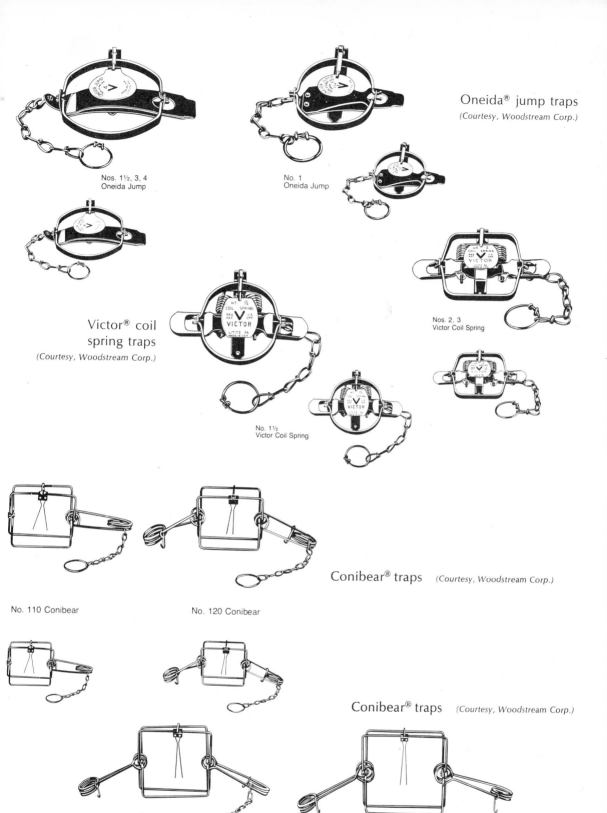

Oneida® jump traps
(Courtesy, Woodstream Corp.)

Nos. 1½, 3, 4
Oneida Jump

No. 1
Oneida Jump

Victor® coil
spring traps
(Courtesy, Woodstream Corp.)

Nos. 2, 3
Victor Coil Spring

No. 1½
Victor Coil Spring

Conibear® traps   *(Courtesy, Woodstream Corp.)*

No. 110 Conibear

No. 120 Conibear

Conibear® traps   *(Courtesy, Woodstream Corp.)*

No. 220 Conibear

No. 330 Conibear

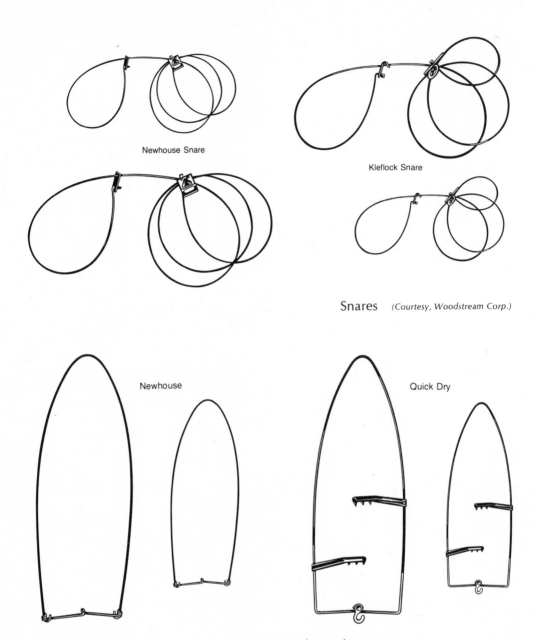

Newhouse Snare

Kleflock Snare

Snares   (Courtesy, Woodstream Corp.)

Newhouse

Quick Dry

Fur drying frames   (Courtesy, Woodstream Corp.)

animals. The best use for these is the live trapping of pests around farms and even urban city lots. Woodstream Corporation now manufactures a fold-up live trap for use by gardeners, farmers, and youth groups. A well-established name in humane live traps is Havahart, made by Allcock Manufacturing Company.

Specialized killer-type traps for moles and gophers are available and are discussed in Part Two.

Muskrat Traps

When using the steel leg-hold trap for muskrat, the sure-grip or stop-loss type should be used in either the underspring or longspring model. Muskrats are notorious for twisting out of traps. These traps feature a delayed action spring that slams forward and pins the muskrat down after he has been caught in the trap's jaws; sometimes it even kills the animal outright. Held fast, the muskrat who survives the initial blow of the spring quickly drowns, even in shallow water. If using conventional leg-hold traps, preferably in sizes No. 1 or No. $1\frac{1}{2}$, make every effort to anchor the traps in deep water. This will help drown the muskrat quickly. The floating raft set, described in the section on muskrats, is one of the sets where the conventional leg-hold trap can be used effectively in drowning muskrat. The body-grip trap in sizes No. 110 or No. 120 in Victor Conibear or No. 1 in Blake & Lamb is fine for muskrat, particularly in the entrance to an underwater tunnel. If the muskrat is not killed instantly it quickly drowns.

Mink Traps

Leg-hold traps most suited for mink are the No. $1\frac{1}{2}$ coilspring and the No. $1\frac{1}{2}$ underspring in Oneida Victor or Blake & Lamb and body-grip traps in the No. 1 by Blake & Lamb or No. 110 or No. 120 Victor Conibear.

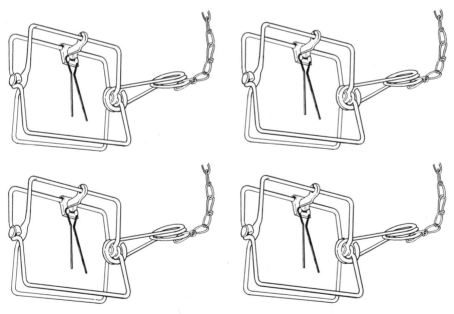

The Blake & Lamb No. 1 sure-grip trap is a favorite for mink and muskrat.   *(Courtesy, Blake & Lamb, Inc.)*

The Bigelow humane trap is
another style of killer-type
trap. *(Courtesy, Bigelow Humane
Trap Co.)*

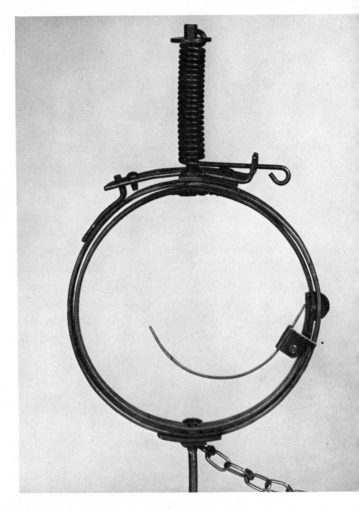

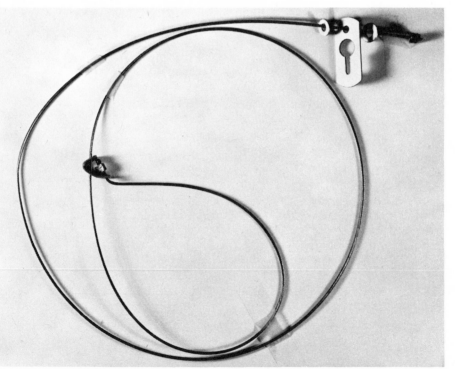

The Thompson
locking snare,
vorite of Cana
and northcoun
trappers. *(Cou
Raymond Thompson (*

Other Traps

Leg-hold traps in No. $1\frac{1}{2}$ in longspring, underspring, and coilspring models are used for a variety of furbearers including mink, muskrat, weasel (larger than needed but will catch a weasel high across the shoulders and kill instantly), skunk, oppossum, raccoon, and marten.

Probably the most popular trap for fox trapping is the Victor coilspring No. 2. It is also a favorite for raccoon, but many prefer the Victor coilspring No. $1\frac{1}{2}$ for raccoon.

The No. 3 size trap in longspring, double longspring (greater holding power), and underspring is used for fox, coyote, otter, badger, fisher, bobcat, and lynx. The No. 4 size is recommended for beaver, wolf, and wolverine.

Traps are sold at hardware and sporting goods stores. They are also available through trappers' supply houses. Look for their ads in the magazine *Fur-Fish-Game*. This national magazine can be found on newsstands and is available through subscription. It is the only major magazine that caters to trappers and has a long and colorful history. *Fur-Fish-Game* is located at 2878 E. Main St., Columbus, Ohio 43209.

Among the well-established trappers' supply houses are Hawbaker, E. J. Dailey, O. L. Butcher, Cronk's, and Northwoods Trapline Supplies. There are many more. Most offer catalogues of trapping supplies including a fascinating array of scents, lures, and baits, and nothing is quite so enthralling as browsing through their pages in the off-season.

Specialized Equipment

Various items are required by the trapper, particularly the fox, coyote, wolf, and wildcat trapper. A packbasket or backpack for carrying traps and other equipment. A hatchet for cutting and driving stakes. Small shovel or gardener's hand trowel or both for digging trap beds and making artificial hole sets. Gloves, either rubber or cotton for land trapping, and elbow-length rubber gloves for making water sets. Trap pan covers: 6–8″ square of light canvas with a slit cut from one edge to center to allow the trigger to fly when the trap springs. Others prefer wax paper as a trap cover. A dirt sifter made from $\frac{1}{4}$″ wire mesh (for covering traps in fox and coyote trapping), about 1′ long x 1′ wide with a wooden frame. Wax and wood dye for coloring, deodorizing, and preserving the life of steel traps. A wide range of scents, lures, and bait.

Grapples

A grapple is a two-pronged affair that looks like two giant fishhooks back to back. It has at least four feet of extension chain that is wired or linked to the trap chain. Steel grapples are considered superior to stakes by many coyote and wolf trappers, since these animals are powerful and

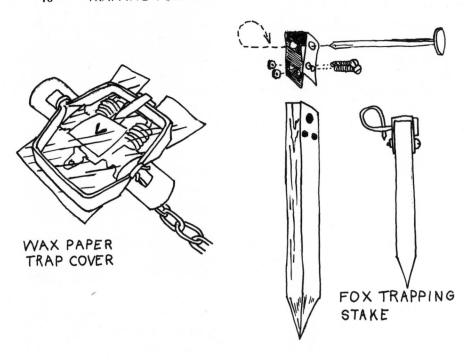

WAX PAPER
TRAP COVER

FOX TRAPPING
STAKE

difficult to hold in a solidly staked trap. They are also occasionally used by fox and bobcat trappers, particularly in the winter months when it is not easy to pound a stake into the ground. The grapple and extension chain is buried beneath the trap and, when a coyote or wolf is caught, the animal is able to leave the set location but becomes entangled on entering thick cover. A coyote or a wolf is a powerful animal but it cannot exert its full strength against a grapple as it can against a solidly staked trap. The grapple continually becomes snagged, unsnagged, then resnagged again, although it is usually firmly hung up by the time the trapper arrives. Grapples can be bought commercially but most trappers prefer to make their own. Coyote and wolf grapples are generally about 9″ long x 7″ wide and made of $\frac{3}{8}$″ or better steel.

Stakes

Steel stakes are useful for fox trapping and can be bought commercially but most trappers like to make their own stakes from wood. An excellent stake, usually about 12″ long for clay soil, longer for sand, can be made from old hardwood flooring. A piece of sheet metal is fitted over the top of the stake and held in place with two nuts and bolts to prevent splitting when pounding on the stake. A final touch is to drive a spike through the stake and sheet metal and then form a loop in the pointed end of the spike. The trap chain can be wired to this loop.

The list of trapline equipment can be rounded out with a skinning knife, wire clippers, and hip boots or chest-high waders for water trapping of mink and muskrat. Fox and coyote trappers will want a supply of baits and lures.

The following traps are recommended in jaw-spread sizes:

JAW SPREAD (Approx.)	TO CATCH
$3\frac{5}{8}''$	Barn Rat, Gopher, Weasel
$4''$	Muskrat, Woodchuck, Oppossum, Skunk, Mink
$4\frac{3}{4}''$	Marten, Mink, Skunk, Woodchuck, Oppossum, Fox, Raccoon, Bobcat (small)
$5\frac{1}{2}''$	Coyote, Fox, Beaver, Lynx, Badger, Bobcat, Fisher
$5\frac{7}{8}''$	Otter, Beaver, or Wildcat

2
DYEING and WAXING TRAPS

Successful wolf, coyote, and fox trapping depends to a high degree upon the care and treatment utilized in preparing traps and equipment. Traps must be free of the odors of steel and rust; in fact, they must be free of all odors foreign to the animals sought. This is accomplished by boiling the traps in a solution of water and wood dye. This is an outside job best done over an outside fireplace; you can improvise by placing flat rocks in a U shape and putting several iron bars across the rocks to support the tub.

Dyeing and waxing of traps should be done by all trappers regardless of the animals sought. This prevents rusting and makes traps more operable under conditions of ice and snow. Few trappers are not within the range of mink. While mink may be readily taken in water sets with shiny or rusty traps, a well-blackened and waxed trap free of foreign odor is helpful in land trapping and snowsets for mink.

The first step in treating traps is to boil them for several hours in a tub of water. This will remove oil from new traps and excessive rust and dirt from older traps. Before putting traps into boiling water, first put a nail or trap chain link between the jaws. Later, when wood dye and wax are added, the inside of the jaws will get a good coating of dye and wax. It is handy to fasten a short piece of stovepipe wire to each trap to help with the handling and hanging of the trap. Later, this same wire can be used to load and unload your traps, thus one need not wear clean cotton or rubber gloves. Discard the wire before setting the trap.

After the traps have been boiled for several hours, pour off the oil, dirt, and old wax that have risen to the surface. If traps are new, remove from tub and leave out in the weather for several weeks to rust. It is important that traps have a coating of rust because smooth shiny steel will not take on a good color. If your traps are already rusty, bring clean water to a boil and add about one pound of commercial wood dye to each five gallons of water. You can also use bark to dye traps, such as that from soft maple, white oak, green butternut, sumac bulbs, walnut hulls, or other material or trees common to the area. However, evergreen bark should not be used, it produces an overly concentrated odor.

If time permits, leave your traps set for several days in the water and wood dye solution. This will give the tannic acid in the wood or bark dye time to etch itself into the metal and will give more permanent coloring.

This is as far as many trappers care to go. Traps and other equipment that have been boiled in the dye solution can be removed and stored in a clean, airy place. In a few days they will lose their slightly smoky odor and be ready for the trapline. Some trappers prefer to wax their traps also; this gives the traps extra speed in closing.

To go on to the waxing process, remove traps from the water and allow to dry completely. This is important, wet traps or traps that are hotter than the wax (such as those just lifted from a boiling wood dye solution) will not take a good coating of wax. When traps are perfectly dry, place a bucket of commercial trap wax over a small fire and heat until wax is melted and smoking hot. There must be enough wax to cover a trap completely. Now dip each trap into the wax. Leave the trap in the wax solution a minimum of one minute to ensure that each trap reaches the same temperature as the wax. Pull out the trap, shake off the excess wax, and hang in an airy shed or garage. Steel trap stakes, grapples, hand trowels, and the like should receive the same deodorizing treatment as the traps but it is not necessary to wax these accessories. A substitute for commercial trapper's wax is simply paraffin wax with a pea size drop of pine gum added.

An Alternative to Waxing

Acrylic floor finish, available at grocery stores in either spray cans or gallon liquid containers, has been found by some trappers to be an efficient substitute for wax; the latter can be dangerous to handle when heated. Acrylic floor finish is cheap, safe to use, odorless, easy to apply, and dries to a hard plastic finish that is slick and super fast when the pan drops on a trap so treated. Simply dip traps into a container filled with liquid acrylic or pour the liquid over traps set in a container. The traps are then taken out and dried.

Chapter
3
PRESEASON SCOUTING

To ensure a successful trapping season, get out into the field and scout your proposed trapline before the season opens. In many areas of the United States and Canada, there is only a short time period between when the trapping season opens—or furs become prime for harvesting—and the winter freeze-up. Once the creeks and marshes freeze, water trapping is difficult. It is the same with land trapping. Once there is snow or alternating freezing and thawing temperatures, it is difficult to keep the traps, set for land animals, working. Animals like the raccoon and skunk will hole-up during cold weather. So the first few weeks of the trapping season are very important. To save time and to take best advantage of the first critical weeks of trapping, it pays to know where most of your sets will be made. This is accomplished by preseason scouting.

Late summer and early fall are good times for scouting. A cool, breezy day spent wading a small stream in search of mink, muskrat, and raccoon sign will put almost any trapper into a state of euphoria. It is fascinating and it is fun. One can become so absorbed in examining a possible set location that on rising from a crouched position below a stream bank a fox is seen drifting by only scant feet away, or a mink is sighted working its way towards you. Just the world of tracks and droppings, trails winding through grassy swale, and dark passageways under overhanging banks are heady stuff to the trapper.

Along waterways you can scout for a variety of furbearers, including mink, muskrat, raccoon, beaver, and otter. Frequently, set locations for land animals like fox, coyote, and bobcat can be found near waterways. A log crossing a small stream can—depending on the area—be used by wolf, coyote, fox, bobcat, lynx, wolverine, fisher, marten, raccoon, skunk, oppossum, mink, and weasel.

Scouting for muskrat can get a little confusing if the animals are abundant because it is difficult to keep track of all the sign: tracks, trails, runways, droppings, feed cuttings (bits of roots and stems), underwater tunnels, and houses built of vegetable matter.

Still, you will want to make note of hotspots. Now is a good time to sink rocks (attach a length of stovepipe wire to each) into deep water near these hotspots for use as trap anchors. When the season is open it takes only moments to twist the other end of the wire onto a trap chain. Actually, it can be difficult to find rocks that wire can be wrapped around permanently. One solution is to fill sacks with small stones and tie the sack tops shut with a length of stovepipe wire. Hunks of cement blocks or scrap iron, in addition to stakes driven into the bottom in deep water, can be used to anchor traps. Anchoring traps in deep water not only ensures that a trapped animal quickly drowns, it also helps to prevent a trapped animal from being stolen. A valuable mink caught in one of your traps and struggling in shallow water will attract the attention of passersby—animal or human. A submerged, drowned mink may not be noticed.

The material on mink trapping has details on several sets that can be prepared before the season opens: the artificial hole set, the box cubby set, and the cubby, the latter made from natural materials found at the set location. Prepare these sets at least several weeks in advance of the trapping season to give them a chance to weather and to take on a more natural appearance. If, in time, the artificial hole takes on the appearance of an old, abandoned muskrat burrow and the open-ended cubby looks like the extension of an overhanging bank with exposed tree roots, these sets are more effective.

A lot of human odor is left if much time is spent working on these projects but this will be long gone by the time the trapping season opens. Once the sets have had a chance to "weather" and all trace of human odor dissipated, bait and lure can be added to the artificial hole sets, usually about a week before the trapping season opens. Bait and lure are not used with the cubby sets, which in the case of mink trapping are simply narrow, open-ended passageways meant to arouse a mink's curiosity. However, a few drops of mink urine sprinkled on the inside of the cubby will indicate to an investigating mink that another has passed this way; the sprinkling can lull suspicion, putting the mink at ease and off its guard.

The material on raccoon trapping describes a cubby and an artificial hole. The cubby described—the more common type, used with bait and lure—is a shedlike affair with one end left open for the animal to enter and the trap to be set. These and other sets should be constructed in places where fresh tracks, trails, and droppings indicate that raccoon are active, or where you believe raccoon will be active in late fall when fruits and crops ripen. However, a natural situation is better for raccoon, mink, muskrat, or any furbearer. For example, a natural cleft in a rock formation where bait can be placed and guarded by a trap. It is hard to improve on a natural cubby, hole, or passageway except to put guide sticks in place if necessary. Guide sticks are pieces of dead tree limbs shoved into the stream bottom or ground to force the investigating animal to step where you have set or, in the case of preseason scouting, will set a trap.

A hollow log lying in a shallow stream with a few inches of water running through it is an example of a natural set location that is hard to improve on except that guide sticks might be required to narrow the space where traps are set at either end of the log. During preseason scouting you can give nature a hand by rolling hollow logs found in nearby woodlands into a stream—unless it would better serve your purpose to use the log as a dry land set. You can also reposition a hollow log or stump that is already in a stream. It may be lying too deep or too shallow. Mink, raccoon, otter, even muskrat will investigate such a hollow log for crayfish or other small aquatic life seeking shelter in it.

Carry a notebook for marking down and describing, briefly, the good set locations you find. Later these can be transcribed in a larger notebook kept in your home or car. Handier than a conventional notebook are sheets of paper enclosed in plastic folders. These plastic folders, available at stationery and school supply stores, can be handled with wet and muddy hands.

The sign left by beaver—felled trees, dams, and lodges—is easy to notice. A good indication that a lodge is occupied and the beaver active is fresh mud plastered on the lodge and along the dam or auxiliary dams. When a lodge or dam is long out of use, rain and snow wash away most of the mud packing and leave only bare branches and logs. Grass and weeds grow up from what mud and earth are not washed away.

Otter are fond of beaver ponds and almost any body of water or waterway. If you find an otter slide, and otter trapping is allowed in your area, you have a real hotspot (see the otter trapping section for details). Prior to the season opening it is wise to leave the slide undisturbed. You may wish to prepare a drowning wire or to sink a sack of rocks with wire attached in deep water. Otter are one of the toughest animals to hold in a steel trap. Every effort should be made to drown them.

Try to do your preseason scouting of waterways when water levels are near normal. Scout again, just prior to the opening of trapping. Conditions can change, water levels fluctuate, so a last minute check of conditions will prepare you for any eventuality.

Dave Gilsvik looks over beaver lodge on early winter scouting trip. In many areas, beaver trapping is not open until late winter or early spring.

The trapper who plans to trap fox or combine trapping fox, coyote, bobcat, and lynx along with trapping water animals will find plenty that is fascinating; time spent seeking fresh tracks, trails, and droppings along woods trails, forest clearings, unused pastures, the edges of cultivated fields, and dusty backroads is time well spent. It is best to look after a period of fair weather. Heavy rains or even strong winds in some desert areas might obliterate tracks. Tracks will be more visible in sandy areas or soft dirt. Trappers in the West generally look in dry or sandy arroyos—gullies. Rabbits and other rodents frequent eroded gullies and in turn lure coyote, fox, and bobcat.

Fox like to follow cow paths and will hunt the edges of brushy fencerows. Coyote and fox will both dig for gophers and field mice, so it pays to scout areas that are abundant with these rodents.

Coyote, fox, and cat dung will all show fur, bits of bone, or sometimes fish scales. Ranchers and farmers will often see coyote and fox so it pays to ask around then scout the area where such animals were sighted. At the same time you can be observing likely spots to make sets. Generally, sets for both fox and coyote are made in open fields or clearings with short

17

Rich Gilsvik examines beaver-gnawed tree.

grass and a long view. If the prevailing winds are from the northwest, you will want to consider a dirt-hole set, as described in the material on fox trapping, to the northwest of a fenceline traveled by foxes. Bait and lure are used with this popular set but the bait and lure must be detected by the fox in order to be effective.

It's a good idea to dig dirt-hole sets, a very popular set for fox and coyote, prior to trapping. A week or two before traps are set, bait and lure should be added. One of the secrets of successful trapping is to entice the furbearers to visiting your sets before you actually set the traps. Often just a freshly dug dirt hole is attractive to furbearers. If you've found bobcat sign along an old lumber trail or sandy arroyo, you might want to consider a dirt-hole set along the edge of the lumber road or arroyo or a cubby built nearby. Watch for ravens and buzzards, they can tip you off to the presence of a dead deer or other carrion that will lure bobcat, coyote, fox, wolf, fisher, marten, wolverine, skunk, oppossum, and weasel. Even when only a few bleached bones remain, coyote and fox will remember and return to the bones to sniff around and reminisce about this once easy meal.

Consider scouting for skunk and oppossum dens if fur prices warrant trapping them. (Trapping at dens is not always legal so check local regulations.) Even when prices are low, fair wages can sometimes be made by trapping these prolific animals in large numbers. Baited cubby sets should be constructed near where tracks, trails, and droppings are found. Box cubbies and other sets for weasel are generally put out after snowfalls and weasel tracks are seen. If your trapping grounds are familiar, you are probably aware of spots where weasels frequent.

A challenge to hobby trappers would be to take several furbearers of each type found locally. With the exception of one or two, all will bring some monetary return. For many years the long-furred animals had little or no fur value, but at the time of this writing all furbearers with the exception of skunk and ermine are bringing good prices, and it would not be surprising if skunk and ermine came back in favor. Preseason scouting for a variety of furbearers is challenging and fun . . . and will add to your profits.

Chapter
4
BAIT and LURE

THE function of bait and lure (scent) is to attract the animal's attention and induce it to come close to the set location. Sometimes this inducement is the promise of food, sometimes it is sexual excitement or simply curiosity. Both bait and lure can be bought from supply houses. Many of these manufacturers have been in business for decades. Most are reputable dealers, who are or have been trappers. The prices they charge for their products are reasonable and even the young trapper can afford a bottle or two of lure and perhaps a jar of bait for fox trapping. Bait and lure are especially useful in trapping wolf, coyote, and fox.

Furbearers can be caught without bait or lure in trails, runways, den entrances, or where they enter or leave streams, yet many sets can be improved with the use of bait or lure and a few are wholly dependent upon it.

While the majority of trappers will use commercial lures, many prefer to collect their own bait. Fresh bait is usually preferred for mink, weasel, raccoon, marten, fisher, bobcat, and lynx. Tainted baits are favorites for fox, coyote, skunk, and oppossum. Muskrats like vegetables: carrot, apple, celery, parsnip, green turnip tops, corn, and potato.

The trapper who looks ahead will save flesh of game birds, muskrat, beaver, red fox, and skunk: heads, entrails, feathers, scraps of hide and bone; and fish pieces. These can be kept frozen in plastic bags until needed, then thawed and used fresh or slightly tainted.

Tainted Bait

Late summer and early fall are good times to prepare tainted bait for trapping fox, coyote, wolf, skunk, and oppossum. Depending on where you live, there are usually one or two unprotected species of animal that can be shot and used for bait, including woodchuck, jack rabbit, prairie dog, rock chuck, porcupine, and skunk. Check your local regulations. If, for example, you have shot two woodchucks for bait (a favorite in the East because of the large size and availability) first put the animals in a paper sack to prevent flies from gathering on the carcasses; this keeps maggots out of your bait jar.

In the evening when the flies are less of a problem, take the animals from the bag. Some trappers, careful not to handle the bait with bare hands, use rubber gloves. Remove the entrails and with a hatchet or meat cleaver cut the carcasses into cubes about the size of a walnut. Do not skin the animals and use all but the entrails, feet, and tail. Put the cubes in clean mason jars and screw the lids on tightly. Bury the jars under nine to ten inches of dirt in a cool, shaded spot. After several weeks the bait will be slightly tainted and ready to use. Use one or two pieces to a fox set.

Sometimes beaver and muskrat carcasses can be obtained at fur houses when they are buying spring-caught animals, or the trapper can save a few carcasses of beaver and muskrat that he himself has caught. However, if it is the spring of the year this bait should be kept frozen until September or October, then thaw and use fresh or bury for several weeks as described above. Taxidermists can be a good source of animal or fish flesh. Another source of bait are deer killed on highways. Usually these must first be inspected by a conservation officer (game warden) and any edible meat utilized. Often the animal is so badly damaged that it is discarded. Leave word with a nearby conservation officer that you can use such a carcass for bait. The flesh of domestic animals such as horse, mule, and cow make good bait.

Flesh from red fox can be used fresh or slightly tainted to catch other foxes. It is particularly attractive to grey foxes.

Remember that tainted bait is best when only slightly tainted. If bait gets too ripe the fox or coyote is more inclined to roll in it. Rotten bait tends to lure undesired animals into fox and coyote sets.

Fresh Bait

Mink, raccoon, and oppossum are attracted by small baits of fish, frogs, or crayfish, also fresh pieces of rabbit and muskrat flesh. Canned sardines and salmon can be used. Mice, red squirrels, and other small creatures are good bait when used fresh for mink, fox, marten, and fisher. Feathers or deer hair scattered about a set location will add to its appeal. Weasels like fresh meat and blood; the head and entrails of a freshly killed rabbit are ideal.

Lure

Home lure making is complicated and messy and more often than not the amateur lure maker will end up chasing away more furbearers than he lures in. Commercial lures are reasonably priced and well worth it.

FISH OIL

If you are still set on brewing up a batch of lure you might try making fish oil. Fish oil is not only an important part of many lure formulas, it is also an effective lure when used alone. It is easy to make and is very popular in trapping mink, raccoon, skunk, and oppossum. Start with a clean gallon jar. Half fill the jar with chunks of fish, almost any fatty fish will make good fish oil: carp, suckers, perch, sunfish, eels, or trout. Cover the top of the gallon jar to permit gases to escape but prevent flies from entering the jar. Keep the jar in full sun at all times and away from cats and dogs.

As the solids deteriorate the oil will begin to appear on the surface. After several weeks of "sun rendering," several inches of oil, clear yellow to amber colored, will have risen to the top.

Pour off the oil into a clean bottle. Put your gallon jar back in the sun. It is quite likely that several more ounces will be produced in a few weeks.

More Lures

The following tips on home lure making come from The Trapper Education Program of Manitoba and the Manitoba Registered Trappers Association:

Scents and baits are lures used to attract animals into traps. The scent is more important than the bait because it lasts longer and creates greater curiosity on the part of the animal being hunted.

Mink musk and honey mixed together make a lure which attracts most animals. Mink musk sacs are located at the anus. To prepare this lure, take the musk glands from several mink and either press the musk into one pound of liquid honey or place the glands into one pound of warmed liquid honey. The warm honey will help release the musk from the gland. Stir the honey to ensure that the musk is well mixed in.

Cheap perfume makes a good lure for ermine, and a few drops in a spruce-bough cubby will soon pay off in ermine pelts.

Animal urine, especially from foxes and coyotes, has proven an effective lure for trapping these species. (This can be collected from dead animals: Open the animal with a knife and remove the bladder.) A few drops sprinkled around a set often means the difference between a catch and a miss.

Orange peel is good muskrat lure. Carrots also attract muskrats. Where these are not available, the muskrat musk glands, collected in spring, are as effective as any lure.

Lynx are usually lured quite easily with beaver castor, but we now have the recipe for a much more effective lynx lure, recommended by veteran trapper Ralph Bryenton of Herb Lake:

Rot lynx livers in a jar all summer. Take a pint of this rotted liver and add six drops of aniseed, six drops of valerian, small bit of powdered catnip, and six drops of lynx urine. Throw in about five tablespoonsful of powdered lynx droppings and one finely chopped beaver castor (perineal gland). Mix well. This is one of the best lynx lures invented.

To use this lure, put a daub of it on a 2″ hay ball, tie it to a stick with string that has been saturated in beaver oil and place it at the back of the cubby in an upright position. This will lure lynx into a pen set with either snare or trap. When making lures remember that castor taken from pregnant female beaver is weaker than that from other beaver.

A good mink lure which also attracts most other animals can be made from fish oil. (The making of fish oil is described above.)

An excellent fox lure is lard cracklings. This is the fatty tissue of pork or beef from which the lard has been rendered. After making the set, scatter a few cracklings around in such a manner that the fox must cross and recross the trap while retrieving the lure.

A very good coyote lure can be made as follows: 5 lbs. rotted horsemeat; 20 drops Tonquin (Asiatic) musk; enough glycerine to make a paste. This is especially good in the cold winter months. By adding fish oil and coyote urine you will have a lure good the year round. (Asiatic musk is now made synthetically and can be ordered from drugstores.)

Fish oil with beaver castor makes an attractive lure for fisher. Fisher are generally trapped in pens and a rabbit makes a good bait. Another good fisher lure is: fish oil (1 pint), muskrat musk (2 glands), oil of aniseed (10 drops), Asofetida (10 drops).

A good lynx lure can be made from two dried beaver castors, a small handful of powdered wild catnip, and as much lard as is needed to make a paste. Break open the beaver castors and throw away the covering keeping only the inside. Add the catnip and mix together with lard until it makes a good paste. This lure can be used on scent posts, hay balls, or just about anywhere. The lard helps it last longer.

This recipe can be improved by adding a bit of mink gland and some muskrat musk, which makes it a pretty good mink lure as well.

Wolf, coyote, and fox lures can be made from: four ground-up beaver castors, four (springtime) muskrat glands, six drops of aniseed oil, half a cup of skunk gland, a handful of powdered wild catnip, mink glands (two, if small), a few blades of green grass, about four deer glands (from the legs) and five pounds of meat (deer or similar).

Grind or chop the meat into chunks. Put this into a 4-gallon wooden or glass container. Break or grind up the glands, mix with the catnip and add the meat. If it doesn't mix well, add enough clean fresh water to cover. This should be put aside, covered with a screen, and left to work for the summer. Check it once in a while to see it doesn't get too dry. When it has settled into a well-mixed mass, it can be put into jars, where it will keep for a long time. A bit of this lure will bring coyotes, foxes, and wolves straight in and will attract other animals as well.

Lure is a valuable asset to any trapline but it will not perform miracles. If it's made right, it will draw the desired animal in close to your set and then it all depends on your skill as a trapper. The best set is still one that is attractive to the desired animal, regardless of whether bait and lure are used.

Chapter

5

THE ANIMALS

MUSKRAT

A lowly marsh dweller, a sort of overgrown field mouse, the common and very prolific muskrat is America's leading furbearer. It is also one of the easiest of furbearing animals to catch. Traps need not be concealed for muskrat. It is usually the first animal trapped by youngsters who live within hiking distance of lakes, swamps, or slow moving rivers.

The average muskrat weighs 2–5 lbs and measures 18″–25″ including the tail which is 8″–11″, black, scaly, and flat-sided. This squat little animal has a broad head and tiny eyes. The underfur is dense and waterproof, the guard hairs long and coarse. Fur color is blackish on the back blending to brown, almost reddish tones on the sides with a light, silvery belly. More muskrat are trapped in Louisiana than in any other state, but fur quality is superior in more northerly climes. Each front foot has four clawed toes, each hind, which is partially webbed at the base of the toes, has five clawed toes. In soft mud or snow it is not uncommon to see a drag mark left by the muskrat's tail as well as foot prints.

With the exception of Florida and portions of Texas, California, Alaska, and Canada, the muskrat is found in abundance over North America. In Florida and southern Georgia, the muskrat is replaced by a smaller version called Florida water rat or round-tailed muskrat.

Muskrats are trapped by the thousands each year but trapping seasons are rarely open for more than a two-month period. The gestation period is less than a month and a litter of one to eleven young may appear at any time of the year. It would be hard to find a better example of a renewable resource.

24

A pugnacious and quarrelsome animal, the muskrat will stand up to and even attack a human being when forced into a corner. While many furbearers and predators will cease struggling after a short period in a steel trap, the muskrat will not and by twisting over and over will frequently twist loose. Stop-loss or body-grip traps should be used. The common leg-hold trap can be used successfully if traps are anchored to deep water, thus drowning the animal. This results in more humane trapping as well as less damaged fur for the trapper.

The muskrat is a busy little creature and seems in constant motion. An insatiable eater, diet is dictated by available vegetation: roots and stems of a wide variety of plants, including cattails, bulrushes, and lotuses. This small rodent also eats clams, snails, crayfish, even other muskrats. It may eat its own house if built of tasty roots.

Along streams or lakes with scant vegetation, a muskrat will root out a bank hole. In swamps or lakes with heavy growth of cattails and bulrushes, it commonly builds dome-shaped houses to ensure survival through the winter months. The underwater entrance leads to a spacious chamber. The muskrat's name comes from musk glands located in the groin; they do not have an unpleasant odor.

Trapping methods vary depending on location. A trapper in Louisiana may put in long days poling a small boat through endless marshes making open water sets for muskrat at feed beds and near the muskrat's dome shaped houses. A Minnesota-based trapper may spend his days snowshoeing over frozen, snow-blanketed lakes and marshes setting traps directly in muskrat houses since almost no other sets are possible. Before setting traps in or near muskrat houses, check your local regulations.

In many localities within the United States and Canada, muskrat are trapped in open water sets along creeks, rivers, and marshes early in the trapping season. After the winter freeze, trapping is in under-ice sets or in muskrat houses and push-ups (small houses used mainly as breather holes).

In yet other localities, particularly in Canada, muskrat are trapped during the spring season.

Because muskrat pelts are worth only a few dollars, it takes many pelts to realize a profit, but many hobby trappers set out only a dozen or so traps each season, content to take a modest number of muskrat from a small pond or creek and an unlimited amount of invigorating fresh air and outdoor life. Look for muskrat in almost any water-filled ditch, creek, river, pond, marsh, or lake.

The Floating Raft Set

The floating raft set is made with two logs, approximately 6″ in diameter and 3′ or more in length. These are held together with four cross pieces spiked into the logs, one above and one below, near each end. Two small stakes for bait are forced between the logs and a carrot or slice of apple is impaled on each stake. Three traps are used, one near each end of the raft and one between the two baits. Notches should be cut for the

J. E. Osman   *(Courtesy, Pa. Game Commission)*

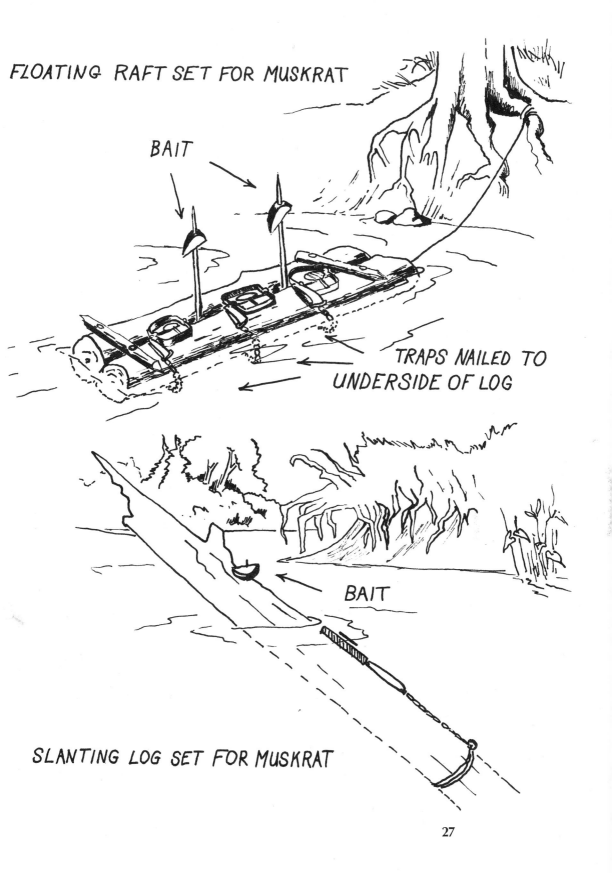

FLOATING RAFT SET FOR MUSKRAT

BAIT

TRAPS NAILED TO
UNDERSIDE OF LOG

BAIT

SLANTING LOG SET FOR MUSKRAT

traps so they will sit level as well as reducing the possibility of their being knocked off. Set in the water, this log raft looks more like a floating snack shop to a hungry muskrat. This is only one of many variations of this set.

Some trappers prefer to make small, single trap models. These can be made at home with old planking instead of logs and can be easily carried. The bait can be impaled on a stiff wire and the wire bent so that the bait hangs right over the trap. Some favor the bait of apple or carrot tied to the pan of each trap—muskrat will reach for the bait with their paws. All seem to work. A commercial muskrat lure can be used with the bait. The biggest asset of this set is that it will remain effective in fluctuating water levels. It is a favorite of springtime trappers where heavy rains or flooding change water levels. It is popular with those who trap large rivers and streams where heavy rains or dams vary the water level. Along a river bank the raft can be tied to an overhanging tree limb or root, or anchored to the bottom in a shallow lake or stream if enough slack is allowed for rising water.

Even without bait, a muskrat can be taken with this set because it likes to climb onto floating logs and debris to rest and eat a mouthful of food at leisure. The steel leg-hold trap can be used with this kind of set. Traps should be anchored to the *underside* of the logs. When a trapped muskrat dives off the raft, the weight of the trap quickly drags it underwater where it drowns. Double and triple catches can be made in one night if a number of traps are used.

The Slanting Log Set

Most streams and lake shores have logs slanting up out of the water, usually from trees that grew on the bank then toppled into the water. The trap should be set a few inches below the water level and wired to the underwater end of the log. Small nails can be used to hold the trap in position. This is a good drowning set and should be baited with apple, celery, or carrot. The bait can be nailed to the log a few inches above the water, and a commercial muskrat lure can be used just above the bait. This set is also good for raccoon.

The Overhanging Bank Set

A muskrat feels at ease swimming in the shelter of overhanging banks where the odds of being spotted by a hunting hawk or owl or being pounced upon by a mink lying in wait along the stream's edge are lessened. This is a good location for a body-grip trap. Select a spot where the trap can be set right up against the undercut bank but still be in five or six inches of water. The stake holding the trap acts as a guide. A cruising muskrat will swim between the stake and the stream bank—and into the trap. Additional guide sticks can be placed farther out in deep

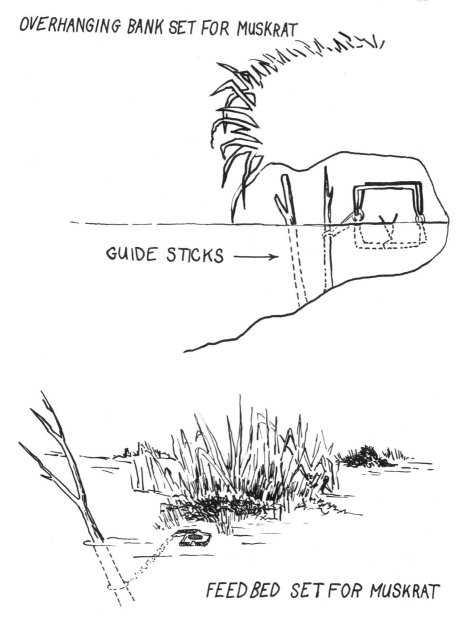

OVERHANGING BANK SET FOR MUSKRAT

GUIDE STICKS →

FEEDBED SET FOR MUSKRAT

water to discourage muskrat from circling around the trap. Mink will also tumble to this set. If there is sign of chewed roots and stems under the bank, set traps on either side of the feeding area.

The Feedbed Set

This is a favorite set of trappers in moderate climates where there is not the constant threat of still and stagnant waters freezing. By cruising in

The author removing muskrat from trap. This prime muskrat was taken in a feedbed set.

a John or other flat-bottomed boat or canoe along the edges of open water in marshes and swamps, the trapper can find many feedbeds (where muskrat gather to eat) in areas where muskrat are active; traps are set under a couple inches of water by these feeding areas, which are identi- fied by fresh root and stem cuttings. Sometimes these masses of feed are actually floating. If the water is shallow, it will pay to lengthen trap chains so the trapped muskrat can reach deep water, or use a stop-loss trap. Body-grip traps can also be used where trails or channels formed by the feeding muskrat lead to the feed pile.

Underwater Tunnel Set

Muskrat frequently live in bank tunnels, the entrances to which are underwater. This is a natural for the body-grip trap. A conventional trap placed in the entrance to such a tunnel will often miss a swimming muskrat or it will be caught by the belly fur and escape, but a body-grip trap is successful almost every time. These underwater tunnels are not easy to find. In a creek or shallow stream it is best to wear hip boots and wade in search of these tunnels. Along lake or pond shores, the trapper can sometimes see long furrows in the bottom where muskrat has passed many times in approaching an underwater tunnel that is just out of sight under the bank. Often, the trapper's foot caves in the tunnel on high ground.

Muskrat House Set

Check local regulations before setting a trap in or near a muskrat house. The important thing in trapping a muskrat house in cold climates is to seal the house properly after setting or pulling a trap. First, use a hatchet to cut a hole in the side of the house, make the hole large enough to get an arm through, then feel around for a dry nest in the house where the muskrat has been resting. This is where the trap is set. Near the nest will be a tunnel of open water leading out below the house and under the ice. Before placing a trap, the trapper should first lift several handfuls of wet vegetation from the interior of the house and set to one side. After setting his trap—preferably a stop-loss or sure-grip trap in size No. 1 or $1\frac{1}{2}$—the trapper should replace the frozen clods of vegetation chopped loose when cutting into the house, then smear the wet vegetation removed from the interior of the house over these replaced clods. In subzero temperatures the wet vegetation will quickly freeze and seal the house and prevent the open water inside from freezing. This situation would trap muskrat below the ice.

The end of the trap chain is attached to a long stake propped outside of the house. It is not necessary to drive this stake into the muskrat house or snow because the muskrat, in trying to escape, will always go for the escape tunnel inside of the house. The long stake cannot be pulled into the house. If using conventional leg-hold traps, be sure to add several feet of wire to the trap chain to allow the muskrat enough slack to dive into its escape tunnel and drown. The body-grip trap can be used in a muskrat house by propping the trap up with sticks by the interior tunnel.

BODY GRIP TRAP

UNDERWATER TUNNEL SET FOR MUSKRAT

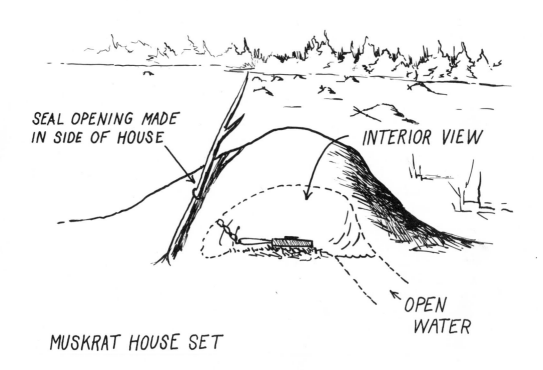

SEAL OPENING MADE
IN SIDE OF HOUSE

INTERIOR VIEW

OPEN
WATER

MUSKRAT HOUSE SET

Baited Body-Grip and Rat Traps

The old fashioned snap-type rat trap is a killer-type trap that has been around a long time but which has received little notice from fur trappers. Not only will it kill common brown rats, it will be as effective on muskrat, weasel, gopher, and other small game—and with an economical price tag. It will also break your fingers. Be careful with this little trap.

When the wood on these traps stays damp for a long time, the spring tension causes some of the staples to pull loose. This can be remedied by pulling the staples, boring the holes completely through the trap and replacing with loops of wire. Two holes should then be bored near the center of the trap and, when making a set, soft wire run through these holes and around a stake that has been pushed into the mud bottom of a lake or pond. Have the trap set so the baited trigger is facing down and about four inches above the water. For bait use apple, carrot, or celery. Put a few drops of muskrat gland lure on top of the trap. The muskrat will reach for the bait with his mouth and be killed instantly.

The body-grip trap works in much the same way. In either case, the placement of the set is important. The nearer the sets are made to known muskrat travel routes, the better will be the catches.

Muskrat can be trapped in trails and runways and where it has been noted that the animals are crawling onto land or onto rocks and logs. Look for droppings, tracks in soft mud, and signs of feeding. Mink trappers are forever having muskrat stumble into sets made around exposed tree roots at water's edge and other passageways investigated by

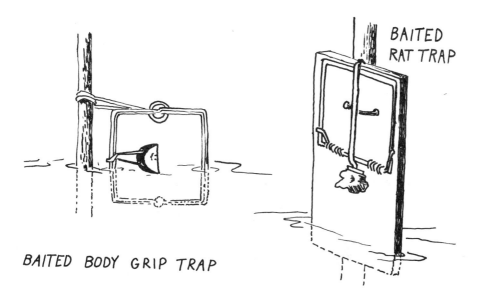

BAITED RAT TRAP

BAITED BODY GRIP TRAP

both mink and muskrat. Fortunately the mink and muskrat seasons are usually open simultaneously so both furbearers are utilized.

Favorite traps for muskrat are the No. 1 and 1½ stop-loss or sure-grip in either longspring or underspring models. Body-grip traps are the No. 110 or 120 in Victor Conibear or No. 1 Blake & Lamb. Muskrat are case-skinned (in case-skinning, the trapper makes a cut from one hind foot to the other and removes the pelt like a glove). Wire fur stretchers are favored for muskrat but wood stretching boards can be made. These are usually 24″ in length, ¼″ thick, 7″ wide at the base, 6″ wide at the shoulder.

MINK

For many trappers the mink is the most coveted prize on the trapline. Mink have retained a high market value for the last half century. Young trappers, while able to take a fair number of the more common and prolific muskrat, will dream of the day they take their first mink. One mink pelt may equal the market value of a dozen muskrat. Yet it is not so much the market value as it is a sense of outfoxing a more difficult quarry. For the mink is a hunter with keen senses.

Mink need not be difficult to trap, particularly in the fall when the trapping is done in conditions of open water. Later in the season, when the creeks and marshes freeze over and snow blankets the northern range of the mink, this little furbearer does become a difficult quarry.

Mink are widely distributed throughout North America from the Gulf of Mexico to the Arctic Circle and from Labrador south to Florida. The

mink falls into one of the four main groups of which the weasel family is divided according to body structure. It has the typical slender mustelines of the marten and weasel. Science recognizes eleven subspecies, the largest of which is found in Alaska and the Yukon. All varieties or subspecies are similar and will have body lengths of 18″ to 24″ including their 8″ tails. Weight varies from 1–3 lbs. Mink pelts become prime—suitable for harvesting and marketing—in November. Generally the mink found in the southern regions of the United States have a poorer quality fur and lighter color than the dark brown mink found in the northern regions of the United States and Canada. About 1,000,000 mink are trapped each season, and another 5,000,000 are raised by America's 5,000 mink ranchers.

Like most members of the weasel family, the mink is a solitary wanderer. Savagely aggressive, it seeks its own kind only during spring mating. Mink will raise their young, which can vary from four to eight in a litter, in a hollow log, abandoned muskrat den (in some instances the mink has killed the residing muskrat), rock pile, or any sheltered, dry nest.

Generally found near water, the mink trails by scent, captures small game and birds and varies his diet with fish, frogs, crustaceans, and other forms of aquatic life. They are known to make occasional forays to hen houses where both chickens and eggs are devoured. A natural killer, the mink is adept at capturing and killing its prey. Like the weasel, the mink can become highly agitated and, if the opportunity arises, kill far more than it can eat. Young mink will return to an unfinished meal, but an old mink often depends solely on making fresh kills. It is because of this that the use of bait, while arousing a mink's curiosity, may not always be effective in trapping mink. The question of the effectiveness of bait in mink trapping is a widely debated one.

Most mink are taken on auto traplines. These are sometimes 100 miles or more in length. The trapper makes his sets by bridges in shallow channels of water between a bridge abutment and the shore, or where he feels mink are entering and exiting a small stream at a roadside culvert or traveling through the culvert. Because of high gasoline prices, this kind of trapping is not as profitable as it once was. A benefit of auto traplines is that it is usually the older, male mink that are caught.

The male mink is the real traveler in the mink family. It may take him a week or more to cover his hunting grounds. The female mink and the young mink of the year stay fairly close to the home den.

Another kind of trapping that takes a lot of mink is boat trapping along major streams. This has the advantage of less competition and, by remaining in his boat while making sets, the trapper leaves less human odor at the set locations. A drawback to boat trapping on a stream of any size is rising and lowering water levels.

Deep-woods trapping for mink is an esthetic experience but generally fewer mink are taken because the trapper is confined to a smaller area.

Where you live and your particular circumstances will determine the kind of mink trapping you do. The preference of many is to seek a compromise. For example, an auto trapline but within a fairly small area and with most sets out of sight of the roadside . . . and possible trap thieves . . . and a few sets in deep woods with some boat trapping for added variety and adventure. Today's trappers are as much in search of the feelings of well-being that accompany trapping as the extra income.

The best places to make mink sets are along the edges of creeks, water-filled ditches, small streams and rivers, marshes, and lake shores. The more fish and aquatic life a stream contains, the more attractive it is to mink.

Scott Gilsvik hefts a mink taken early in the season. Mink are easily trapped when rivers and streams are still open.

The Blind Set

Probably more mink are taken in blind sets than any other. A blind set is simply a trap placed where you believe a mink will step. The favorite set location is a narrow, natural channel between overhanging tree roots and a stream bank. It is the nature of mink to investigate such a narrow passageway. The perfect set would be one just narrow enough to hold the new killer-type, body-grip trap in a size suitable for mink.

WET SET

DRY SET

BLIND SETS FOR MINK

TRIBUTARY

It is this curiosity about every passageway, hole, trail, and tangled pile of flood debris along stream banks that make mink relatively easy to catch, particularly when the trap is set under water. The mink is searching for crayfish and a multitude of other small creatures in these nooks and crannies. A leg-hold trap placed under two inches of water will not give off foreign odor that might otherwise warn a trap-wise mink. If the set location is found before the season opens, the trapper can place a drowning wire in position and have it already anchored to a heavy rock or solidly tied to a stake or tree root. The set can then be quickly made when trapping season opens and little human odor left at the set location.

Trappers can further cut down on human odor at set locations by wearing hip boots or waders and making all sets while standing in the water. Enter and exit a stream some distance up or downstream from set locations. When a set is complete, splash water over the stream bank and the whole set location to wash away any odors you might have left. If using lure, urine, or bait, this should now be placed in a sheltered spot beyond the trap so not to be washed away by rain or snow. Avoid spitting or relieving yourself near set locations. Leave every set looking as natural as you can and free of foreign odors.

There are many variations of the blind set. For example: a hollow log lying in a stream with several inches of water running through it; a stump with a hollow between its roots. Perhaps a portion of bank caved in and a narrow passageway was formed between the clod of earth lying in the water and the remaining stream bank, thus creating a natural blind set. Pockets along stream banks that are formed by trails or draining swamp water entering a stream are investigated by mink. A good set location is where a flowing spring or small brook enters a larger stream. Mink will always explore these tributaries. Generally one does not use bait or lure at a blind set, although some trappers like to use a little mink urine. This is a very natural scent and one that encourages a mink to feel at ease when investigating a stream bank hole, passageway, or trail because it feels another mink has done the same.

The trouble with blind sets is they are rarely perfect. Often there is so much space for a mink to pass through in investigating a hollow log or narrow channel that it may miss stepping in your trap. In this case, guide sticks can be used. These are simply pieces of dead limbs thrust into the stream bottom to narrow the space where a mink can pass, thus the animal is forced into contact with your trap.

Artificial Hole Set

The basic design of the artificial hole set is a dug hole of roughly 6″ in diameter angling upward into a stream bank and then down, or to one side, so the end of the hole is not seen. Mink are curious about all holes along stream banks and are even more so when they cannot see the end. Generally these holes should be dug by the trapper in advance of the trapping season. This set is useful along open stretches of creek or water-filled ditch where little is available in the line of blind sets. The trapper may wish to start putting out pieces of fresh fish bait and, as trapping season draws near, a good commercial mink lure in these holes.

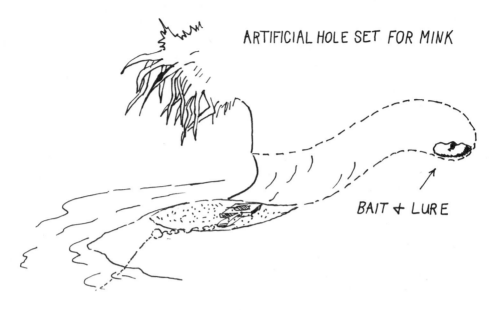

ARTIFICIAL HOLE SET FOR MINK

BAIT & LURE

BOX CUBBY SET FOR MINK

If a mink once starts investigating these holes on its regular rounds, a catch is assured. A good point to remember about baits and lures is that they work best at sets that are attractive to an animal even without bait or lure.

The illustration of the artificial hole set features what is referred to as a "dry land" set because the trap is not under water. Greater care must be taken when making dry land sets. Clean cotton gloves or rubber gloves should be worn. Traps should be darkened and waxed and free of foreign odors (see Chapter 2). The artificial hole set can also be made wet. That is, the hole can be dug at water level, allow a 2″ depth of water at the entrance in which to set the trap. This is an excellent set.

It is wise to use dry sets for about 25% of the sets on one's trapline, including blind sets. That way, if a sudden cold snap should freeze the creek or river you are trapping, these dry land sets will still be operating. Dry land sets should, whenever possible, be sheltered from the elements and completely dry. If the covering of soil, sand, or leaves is not dry, the trap and covering will freeze to the ground in cold temperatures. Even a snow covering should be sheltered because a warm winter sun can cause a dry, powdery snow to thaw. At night, when temperatures plummet, the thawed snow will freeze and your trap won't function.

In making the dry artificial hole set, scatter most of the dirt from the dug hole but leave some in a low heap in front of the hole to give the impression that an animal has been digging. Dig a bed for the trap, so the pan and jaws of the trap are slightly below ground level. Place the trap on a bed of dry grass or leaves. Cut wax paper to fit over the trap so the ends of the paper reach under the jaws on each side. A slot can be torn in the wax paper to allow for the pan trigger mechanism. Now sift fine sand, dirt, or whatever is the natural element at the set location over the trap until it is lightly but completely covered. The wax paper will prevent dirt getting under the trap pan (this could make the trap inoperable). If the set is made under an overhanging bank, it will stay dry in all weather and lessen the chances of the trap freezing down.

The Box Cubby

This is another variation of the blind set but with a helping hand from the trapper. Instead of the space under tree roots or hollow log, we have here a simple, open-ended, rectangular box made by the trapper during his spare time in the summer months and then placed out in late summer or early fall in a likely spot. The box can be wedged against a stream bank so that a couple of inches of water run through the open ends. Logs, debris, or grass can be draped over the box to give it the look of a natural passageway. You can go a step further and blob mud or sand in the bottom of the box cubby to enhance its natural look.

The measurements of the box should be roughly 6″ wide by 6″ high, and 3′ in length. Almost any kind of scrap lumber can be used, but avoid painted wood or oil- and gas-stained wood because of any smell. The boxes can be set out several weeks prior to the trapping season to ensure their being free of foreign odor. These can also be used as dry sets just above the water level along stream shorelines. You may wish to sift fine sand a couple of inches deep in the bottom of the box so that good trap covering is always available.

Traps should always be covered in dry sets. In some instances this will be crumbled, dry leaves or grass, or sand . . . whatever the natural conditions at the set location. A word of warning: Do not blob coarse vegetation over a trap. Leaves, grasses, and weeds should be shredded so as not to plug the action of the trap. Some trappers save a supply of lawn clippings. When dry, this is excellent trap covering for those conditions when dry vegetation is the natural trap covering to use. Use only enough to conceal the trap.

Traps set in water need not be covered. However, if one is using shiny, unblackened traps, it is wise, when possible, to push these into a liquid mud bottom. This makes them almost invisible yet they remain operable. Frequently a shiny, unblackened trap will fool mink in a water set, but why take chances? Have your traps ready for every and all conditions.

Good leg-hold traps for mink are sizes No. $1\frac{1}{2}$ and No. 2 in the handy underspring model or the somewhat more bulky longspring model in the same sizes. A body-grip trap for mink would be the Blake & Lamb No. 1, a killer-type.

Mink should be case-skinned. Wire, commercially made mink stretchers can be used. If you make wood stretchers—which many prefer for mink—they should be roughly $\frac{3}{8}''$ thick, 36'' long, and taper from 4'' at the base to 3'' at the shoulder; sandpaper smooth. Fur buyers generally like the tail split, then held flat on the board with a piece of mesh screen. Adjustable boards are made by some trappers but others find it easier to use a sanded tongue of wood insert to make removal of a dried pelt easier. Slide the insert between the belly fur and the board. Later, when the pelt has dried, the insert is removed and the pelt easily removed from the board.

WEASEL

The weasel is the smallest of the furbearing animals sought by the trapper. He has little fear of traps, or anything else for that matter, and will scramble onto the pan of an unconcealed trap if fresh bait is offered. The elements, however, are in his favor. Trapped almost exclusively during the cold winter months, it is difficult to keep traps set for weasel operating because of snowfalls and alternately freezing and thawing temperatures. The least weasel, the smallest of the three kinds of weasel, is 7''–8'' long and weighs only 1–2 ozs. A steel trap, stiffened by cold, can fail to function under its feathery step. Even the long-tail weasel, 13''–18'', weighs a mere 6–9 ozs.

The long-tail weasel is found in all of the contiguous forty-eight states, most of Mexico, and all Canadian provinces adjacent to the United States.

The short-tail weasel (8″–13″ long) is found throughout Canada and Alaska and the northern half of the United States. The least weasel ranges from Alaska to North Carolina. It is not found in the southwestern and northeastern United States. In some areas the three kinds of weasel overlap.

The lengths given for the three kinds of weasel include their tails. They are overall lengths as are those given for other furbearers in this book. The average tail lengths for the three specie of weasel are 4 to 6″ (long-tail), $2\frac{1}{4}$ to 4″ (short-tail) and 1 to $1\frac{1}{2}$″ (least weasel).

In winter the brown summer coat is shed for a soft, luxurious fur that is pure white except for a black-tipped tail. This white winter fur is called "ermine" and has long been associated with royalty. The robes for a British coronation are reputed to have required more than 50,000 ermine skins.

The weasel's gestation period may be as long as ten months and as many as thirteen young are born in a hollow log, rock crevice, woodpile, or almost any sheltered, dry nest. Always hungry, almost always trying to appease that hunger, the weasel will hunt day or night. Front and hind feet have five toes and their tracks are not unlike that of the mink. Generally little detail shows of weasel tracks in snow. Both front and hind feet land in the same depression and leave two $\frac{1}{2}$″ indentations in the snow somewhat off-center of one another. Each set of tracks is spaced 10″–18″ apart.

In their habits the three kinds of weasel are alike, hyperactive, savagely aggressive, feisty little demons with a very low level of fear. Pursued by a red fox, a weasel often stands its ground against the much larger opponent. Foxes and other large carnivores commonly kill weasels on contact,

usually biting off the weasel's head and leaving the animal uneaten. This may be because they consider the weasel a competitor for food—mice, rabbits, and so forth. Death to mice, rats, gophers, small animals, and birds, the weasel is so horrifying to its prey that a fast-stepping cottontail rabbit can lose control of its limbs and with piercing screams of terror await the weasel's death-dealing bite to the base of the skull.

Look for tracks in the snow in grassy ditches, fencelines, cattail swamps, almost anywhere that high weeds and grass with the resulting field mice and other small animal life are found.

Trail sets or blind sets are rarely effective for weasel. To catch weasel, the trapper must rely on the weasel's sense of smell and lure it into a trap with bait, usually fresh—a little tainted will work. Half a fresh, bloody rabbit is good bait. In northerly areas, trappers will keep snares out for snowshoe rabbits to provide a supply of fresh bait. This is illegal in most areas, so trappers should check with meat markets and meat processing plants for scraps for bait. Almost any kind of animal flesh or offal will attract weasel. It is advisable to use a large piece of bait, as baits and lures give off little odor in cold weather. Make sets only where tracks are found. A weasel must pass fairly close to your set to smell the bait. Once it gets wind of your bait that pelt is as good as on the drying board provided that your trap is not frozen to the ground or a mouse or shrew has not been caught first, attracted by the same bait used to lure the weasel.

The No. 0 trap would seem the likely choice for weasel, but it is pointless to buy traps specifically for weasel since by midwinter the seasons on mink and muskrat are over and mink and muskrat traps can be used for weasel. Besides, a weasel caught in a No. 0 trap will struggle and invariably get urine stains or blood on its fur. These are difficult to remove. On the other hand, a weasel trapped in a No. 1½ underspring will be caught high across the shoulders and die instantly, a quick, humane death, with no damage to its fur.

In some areas of the United States and Canada, weasels can be found in great numbers, although they do tend to run in cycles. Their numbers will be very high for a few years, then scarce for a few years, then high again, for no apparent reason. When fur prices are high and warrant the time and effort, trappers will catch them by the hundreds from auto traplines, keeping most sets by the roadside in grass- and weed-filled ditches and frozen channels that wind through marshland.

The hobby trapper may prefer to snowshoe with a half dozen traps to some distant area of marshland or dense second-growth that he knows to be attractive to weasel. The spice of walking crosscountry on snowshoes or skis is a very tangible outdoor experience. This is the toughest kind of trapping because the man on foot can't carry much. Box cubbies or tin cans used by auto trappers are too awkward to handle. The trapper must rely on his ingenuity to find natural set locations where trap and bait are sheltered from the elements yet within the range of hunting weasels.

If a snowfall is not in the immediate forecast, the trapper on foot can make a very simple set where weasel tracks are plentiful by simply forming a hole in a snowdrift with his fist and placing bait in back of the hole and trap in front. Before placing the trap, flatten a trapbed in the snow and line with wax paper or dry grass. This will help prevent the trap from freezing to the surface of the snow or frozen ground. No covering is used on the trap. Stick a long pole in the snow and through the trap chain loop so the trap and set can be located and retrieved after a snowfall.

More permanent set locations are to be found in rock and wood piles, in small culverts and drain tiles, or in hollow logs and stumps. The hole in the snow set will sometimes miss weasel because in getting to the bait the weasel will bore its own hole in the snow and approach from the side. They are by no means trap-shy but when it is just as easy to bypass a trap the weasel is inclined to do so.

The Leaning Pole Set

When you find a branch from a fallen tree sticking out of the snow at an angle, nail a piece of fresh rabbit near the end of this natural pole. The trap is set below the bait where it will intercept the weasel as it climbs up the slanting pole. The trap can be held in place with nails. While exposed to the elements, the leaning pole set does illustrate the kind of set, easily found, that forces a weasel to first enter the trap jaws when approaching the bait.

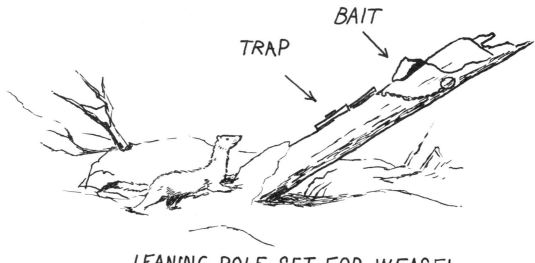

LEANING POLE SET FOR WEASEL

You can tie bait to the pan of a trap and hang or nail the trap on the side of a tree or fence post eight to ten inches off the ground and have a fairly weatherproof set that is also out of reach of small rodents. The weasel, in lunging for the bait, is killed instantly when the trap jaws close around its head and neck. However only a small bait can be used on the trap pan and the set does attract birds.

A slab of bait hanging a foot above the snow with a trap set directly below on a tuft of dry grass is another very simple set that will take weasel. In fact, there are endless variations of simple sets but most have the flaw that they can be put out of commission during adverse weather. The following is a sure-fire set for all kinds of weather.

The Box Cubby

The box cubby is made roughly 6″ wide by 6″ high and 12″ long, with a 2″ hole bored in the front. It looks like a bird house. It can be made from scrap lumber or slab wood which is sometimes free from sawmills. The cover is held in place by a single nail at one end so it can be swung to the side to place the bait and trap and to retrieve trapped weasel. The trap is placed below the 2″ entrance hole and the bait in back of the cubby. The trap chain can be stapled to the cubby or two holes can be bored in the bottom of the cubby and the trap chain anchored with a loop of soft wire through the holes. Actually, it is not necessary to anchor the trap in this set. It is pretty difficult for a trapped weasel to go anyplace.

Because they are cumbersome, box cubbies are set close to the roadside and if put on hummocks of snow or in the shelter of overhanging banks they will remain in working condition even after heavy snowfalls. For serious weasel trapping this set is hard to beat.

The Tin Can Set

This set works best with a tin can that is large enough in diameter to hold a trap in the open end. The can is placed on its side with bait in back and the trap set inside the open end. Weasel have no choice but to step in the trap while reaching for the bait. Cans set in sheltered nooks, under overhanging banks, or in culverts remain in working condition for long periods. This set can be made very quickly and is second only to the box cubby.

Because of low ermine prices in recent years, little experimenting has been done with the body-grip trap in taking weasel. It holds many possibilities. If the trap is kept above the snow level it will work under pretty adverse conditions. Bait can be used directly on the trigger. Another trap worth exploring is the common snap-type rat trap. The only flaw in the rat trap is the small pan, which holds only a tiny bait.

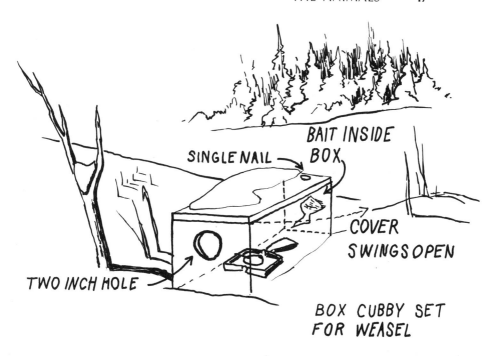

SINGLE NAIL

BAIT INSIDE BOX

COVER SWINGS OPEN

TWO INCH HOLE

BOX CUBBY SET FOR WEASEL

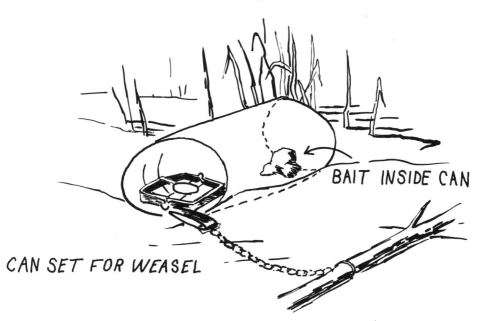

BAIT INSIDE CAN

CAN SET FOR WEASEL

However, the bait pan can be enlarged by attaching a piece of cardboard or mesh screen. When wired or nailed to a fence post or tree trunk in an area of high weasel activity, it is effective. Commercial weasel lure can be used at all sets.

For fast kills use the No. 1½ size underspring trap for weasel. Body-grip traps suitable for weasel are the No. 110 Victor Conibear, No. 1 Blake & Lamb, and the snap-type rat trap. Weasel are case-skinned. Wood fur stretchers should be about 20″ long, ¼″ thick; 2″ wide at the base, 1¾″ at the shoulder. Make a smaller size, as the adult least weasel is very small. Use a board size 20″ long, ¼″ thick, 1¾″ wide at the base, 1½″ at the shoulders. The weasel's tail is not split.

RACCOON

Big, robust, and well furred, the raccoon is a favorite with trappers. This intelligent animal is relatively easy to trap. But there are problems. For example, a trapper will set his traps along a streamside where he has seen heavy raccoon sign during the summer months yet have little success because the raccoons have left the waterways in the fall to scour the wooded ridges and hillsides for beechnuts, acorns, wild cherries, apples, as well as field and sweet corn. In many areas of North America there is only a short time period to take raccoon with prime fur before the animals go into semihibernation. So there are problems involved with raccoon trapping but they add to the interest and challenge of pursuing this colorful furbearer. A point to remember is that the best raccoon trappers use baited woodland sets in addition to streamside sets.

The raccoon's overall body length (including tail) may reach 40″ and weight top the 35 lb. mark. A powerful animal and terrific scrapper, it has been known to maul trailing hounds severely and even to drown a hound by holding the dog's head under water while they struggle in a river or pond. The raccoon has two very distinguishing characteristics, a bandit's mask and a thick bushy tail, 8″–12″ long, with alternating rings of yellowish white and black. The general coloration is a grizzled grey. Nose and ears are pointed, the feet long and slender with naked soles. Each foot has five toes. The raccoon's front feet are unusually nimble, it can easily handle clams and other small objects with its "hands." The hind footprint resembles that of a human infant.

Hunted as well as trapped, the raccoon continues to prosper and even increase its range. Today it is found from the southernmost reaches of Central America throughout some part of each of the contiguous forty-eight states and in every province of Canada bordering the United States. The gestation period for raccoon is sixty-three days, mating occurs in February or March. (In northern areas of the United States and in Canada, the tracks of raccoon will suddenly appear in the snow during this period, especially following mild weather.) The litter varies from two to four. The den is generally a hollow tree but many a dry, sheltered nook is used.

Right from the start the young raccoons get into everything, a habit

(Courtesy, F. R. Martin)

that continues throughout their busy and always curious lives. They are fond of partially cleared farmland in areas of broad-leafed trees. While found in woods and fields, even deserts, they are rarely far from water. There is usually a stream, swamp, or lake within the mile or so diameter of the raccoon's territorial limit.

The raccoon is omnivorous: nuts of all kinds, berries, seeds, corn, honey, crayfish, crabs, clams, oysters, frogs, fishes, small animals and birds, insects, reptiles, chickens and ducks, and eggs of all kinds, including those of the farmer's hens. A nuisance in the farmyard and corn field, a family of raccoons can completely wreck a gardener's patch of corn in one night.

Raccoon are sometimes trapped on long auto traplines. More often the trapper after fox and mink finds that those traps also take raccoon. The dirt-hole set commonly used in fox trapping will lure raccoon, so will some mink sets. Boat trapping, particularly on large southern streams, is a favorite of serious raccoon trappers. Sets are made along the river's edge and also in adjacent fields and woodlands. The hobby trapper will find a short boat trapline an interesting outdoor experience, since mink and muskrat will also be found along the trapline, and perhaps fox in adjacent fields, an interesting combination of trapping which can make this a memorable trapline.

Traps set for raccoon should not be staked solid but rather should be attached to a pole drag. This is usually a 2″ thick length of hardwood tree sapling 10′–12′ long. If the trap is wired about 3′ from one end of the drag, the drag will act like a spring and prevent the raccoon from getting a solid pull and yanking his foot free. In wooded terrain a raccoon will not get far before tangling up and is easily found by the trapper. Be certain to use a hardwood drag—raccoon easily chew through a softwood drag.

The Dirt-Hole Set

To make a dirt-hole set for raccoon, follow the instructions for fox; however, a pole drag is used for raccoon. It is not necessary to place sets in open fields and clearings as one must for the trap-shy red fox. In fact, the dirt-hole set made on a river sandbar as illustrated is a good one for raccoon. The hole is dug at an angle 3″ to 4″ wide, 7″ to 8″ deep. Make a bed for the trap and, if the sand is damp, line the trap bed with a piece of wax paper. Put another piece of wax paper over the trap pan and extending under the trap jaws. A slit is torn in the wax paper to allow the trigger to fly free. Bait of fish or animal flesh should now be placed in the hole and lightly covered. Bait can be fresh or slightly tainted. Sift sand over the trap until it too is lightly covered yet level with the surrounding sand. Put a few drops of commercial raccoon lure (or whatever amount is called for in the directions on the bottle) in the hole and on the back edge of the hole. A few scratch marks over the buried trap will improve the

BAIT IN HOLE

CONCEALED TRAP

DIRT HOLE SET FOR RACCOON

POLE DRAG

BAIT IN BACK

EXPOSED ROOTS SET FOR RACCOON

TRAP UNDER TWO INCHES OF WATER

natural appearance of the dirt-hole set which is an imitation of where an animal has cached a bit of food. The drag can be left exposed.

To prevent the raccoon from digging at the backside of the dirt hole, you can make the hole against a small rock or stump or even use the trap drag as a backing. This same set can be made in fields and woodlands, even the edges of corn fields, *wherever* fresh raccoon sign is found. It is also effective for mink.

The Hollow Stump Set

The hollow stump set is one of many natural set locations one can find in fields and woodlands and along river banks. They are good spots to use a combination of bait, lure, and trap. The stump or hollow log or similar natural cubby provides shelter for the trap from the elements and is itself interesting to raccoons and other wildlife. It is only necessary to cover the trap lightly with leaves or fine wood material found at the set location and to be certain that any raccoon investigating the bait must first pass over the trap. Guide sticks can be used or rocks or other natural material found at the set location to narrow an entrance way. The bait is normally tossed into the back of the hollow stump but a variation is to dig a dirt-hole set right in the hollow stump. The dirt hole is made as already described; in this case, however, it is sheltered from the elements.

A good way to get fresh fish bait for raccoon trapping, and mink trapping too, is to ask bait dealers to save you their dead minnows. Wrap these in plastic bags and freeze until the trapping season. Sardines and other strong smelling canned fish, as well as sweets like jams, jellies, honey, and peanut butter, will lure in raccoon.

Exposed Roots Set

Along any river or stream bank you will find where tree roots have been exposed. Frequently there will be sufficient space under such roots to put a bait of fish, animal flesh, or sweets. The trap should be set under two inches of water and guide sticks or rocks so arranged that the raccoon must step into the trap when investigating the bait. This is also a good bet for mink when fish bait or fresh muskrat flesh is used.

Cubby Set

Cubbies are built like a miniature shed with one end left open for the raccoon to enter and the trap to be set. Entrance to the cubby should be at least 12″ wide and 12″ high. The cubby should be at least 2′–3′ in length and can be constructed of rocks or logs or a combination of material found at the set location. Bait is tossed into the rear of the cubby and the trap lightly concealed in the entrance. Trap should be attached to a hardwood drag. This is a good bet for trapping raccoons when hollow stumps or logs or other natural cubbies are not available. They should be built before the trapping season opens. You can begin baiting and using lure at these sets a few weeks prior to trapping. A good location for a cubby is near a garbage dump, where the raccoon—like the black bear and skunk—likes to rummage for goodies.

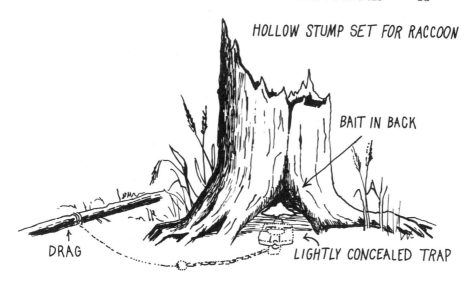

HOLLOW STUMP SET FOR RACCOON

BAIT IN BACK

DRAG

LIGHTLY CONCEALED TRAP

BAIT IN BACK

DRAG

CUBBY SET FOR RACCOON

Artificial Hole Set

Several weeks before the trapping season opens, artificial holes should be dug for raccoon trapping in stream and river banks. Make the holes about 1′–2′ in diameter and at least 2′ deep. Keep the back of the hole dry so bait of fish or animal flesh can be placed there. The entrance to the hole should have a 2″ depth of water in which the trap is later set. After digging this hole, splash water in and all around it. This will smooth the rough edges and very quickly "weather" the hole. A good raccoon lure will improve the set, which also takes mink and muskrat.

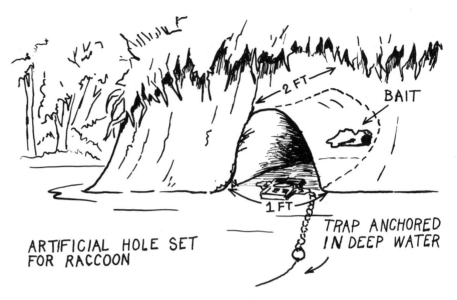

ARTIFICIAL HOLE SET
FOR RACCOON

TRAP ANCHORED
IN DEEP WATER

Raccoon can be taken in blind sets along creek and stream edges where their tracks are easily seen in mud and sand, and show where the animals enter and leave the water, crawl onto logs or rocks, or take shortcuts overland at sharp bends in the creek or stream. Raccoon will wade in shallow water in search of crayfish, frogs, fish, and other small aquatic life. The trapper can determine where the raccoon must maneuver between a boulder and the stream bank and traps can be set in 2″–3″ of water. Simple bait sets can be made. It is not unusual for a trapper to put a slice of apple on a stick (setting his trap below the apple) for muskrat and catch a raccoon. Logs spanning small creeks are used by raccoon, as well as mink, fox, coyote, and bobcat.

Experienced trappers have found that the No. 1½ coilspring trap is ideal for raccoon when used with a drag. The No. 1½ coilspring is a very strong trap for its size and because it is small, it is difficult for a raccoon to reach under the trap jaws and chew away its toes and escape. The animal will occasionally do this if its foot becomes numb and loses feeling after a time in the trap.

The No. 1½ underspring and longspring are also good traps to use for raccoon when a pole drag is used. If raccoon were trap-shy like coyote and fox, a steel grapple would probably have to be used and buried beneath the trap. However, a long pole lying by the set location does not arouse suspicion. A well-blackened trap set under water need not be covered. Traps set for raccoon on land should have a light covering of dirt, leaves, or grass.

Raccoon are occasionally skinned open and stretched almost square but today most are case-skinned. Wood fur stretchers should be about 40″

long, ½″ thick; 10″ wide at the base, 10″ wide at the shoulder. The raccoon is a fatty animal and all excess fat should be scraped free with a fleshing tool or knife. The tail is split and held flat with small finishing nails.

BEAVER

It seems incredible today, but for three centuries, from the time of Jacques Cartier to Kit Carson, trappers ranged across the North American continent in quest of beaver. The trails they blazed would later be followed by settlers. The search for beaver helped open a continent to civilization and almost eradicated the beaver. Trappers are still questing after this oversized rodent but now follow stringent regulations that require the tagging and inspection by a conservation officer of every beaver pelt sold. The season is closed when beaver numbers are low. Often it is the trappers who demand greater restrictions. Today the beaver is a closely regulated, renewable resource, well established in areas with suitable habitat.

A rodent, the beaver is thought to be an easy animal to trap but an adult beaver can be a tough animal to fool if it has survived one or two toe pinchings, usually the result of inexperienced trapping. In fact, little is easy about beaver trapping. The trapper may have to set his traps under ice and have to shovel through thigh-deep snow just to reach the ice. Beaver is not one of the easiest animals to skin and the fleshing job can take the inexperienced all day and still not be done properly, for every hint of oily fat and gristle must be removed. Traps are heavy, cumbersome, and expensive, and the beaver is a tough customer to hold in even the largest steel trap. So it takes experience and know-how to tackle this largest of rodents.

Overall length can reach 4′ and weight can approach the 70 lb. mark. The average weight is 30–40 lbs. The beaver's tail is broad, flat, and scaly. The guard hairs are a glistening chestnut brown, and the soft, luxurious underfur has a reddish tinge. All four feet have five toes and the hind feet are fully webbed. The beaver's range extends from New Mexico to Alaska but it is not found in the extreme southeastern United States. Beaver breed in January or February and a litter of two to six are born from late March to May. By the end of their first year or early in their second, the young beaver will leave the home water to establish their own home.

The beaver is never far from a wild dash into water. Nose valves shut automatically when it submerges, and oversized lungs permit it to stay under water ten to fifteen minutes. He is the master dam builder, a woodcutter, hauler, architect and mason, active day and night but more so at night. Because it does not hibernate, beaver must store winter food supplies. Short tree limbs are wedged in the muddy bottom of pond or stream near the lodge or bank hole. This food locker can be reached even after the winter freeze.

Beaver favor wooded terrain and create a pond or series of ponds from an insignificant trickle of water. It is not unusual for beaver to build a dam in a roadside ditch and to flood the road. Because they are a nuisance at times, flooding roads and indiscriminately felling trees that are of value to the landowner, limited trapping of nuisance beaver is allowed even when the season has been ordered closed. Trappers can contact their local game law enforcement agency for information on trapping nuisance beaver.

Because beaver colonies can occur almost anywhere, in backwoods terrain or roadside ditch, trappers should make note of beaver sign— felled trees, dams, and lodges—whenever they are afield. Beaver sign will often be noted on hunting or fishing trips. Beaver will occasionally live in bank holes along rivers and streams but here not as much sign is left. The beaver's food consists of the bark, twigs, and even the wood of deciduous trees, with a marked preference for poplars, cottonwoods, willows, and alders. The poplar (aspen) found throughout the northern forested regions of the United States and Canada is probably the most sought after by beaver. In the western and prairie states, cottonwood is often the beaver's choice.

The open season on beaver will vary from late fall to early spring depending on where you live and the management problems. Generally, the beaver season opens in late winter when the countryside is still locked in ice and snow and extends through the spring thaw. This allows under-ice trapping early in the season and open water trapping during the late season.

Because many beaver colonies are located far back in the woods where they are difficult to reach, there has always been a renewable supply of beaver to take over when beaver close to the road have been trapped out. The advent of the snowmobile now makes it easier to reach backwood beaver ponds. Because of this, the snowmobile is not allowed for the trapping of beaver in some areas. In other areas, the effect of the snow-mobile on beaver trapping is being studied and evaluated.

Long auto traplines for beaver are used where trappers are allowed to take large numbers of beaver. Driving at that time of year can be difficult with muddy and flooded roads, so four-wheel drive is usually required. Sets are made close to the road so that many beaver ponds can be trapped. Often there is a limit to the number of beaver that each trapper can take; as a result, trappers restrict their activities to a few beaver colonies. The hobby trapper might choose to snowshoe to a backcountry beaver pond to enjoy the experience of deepwood beaver trapping. Because beaver leave such easily recognizable sign, it is difficult to find a spot to trap beaver that is unknown to other trappers, except in the backcountry.

River traplines are popular. The river systems will be open while many beaver ponds are still locked in ice and snow. Wherever he chooses to trap, the inexperienced beaver trapper will have some difficulty at times in determining the freshness of sign left by beaver. Cuttings left from the previous fall will appear fresh even in the spring of the year. One does not become an expert beaver trapper overnight.

Under-Ice Pole Sets

Late fall and early winter are the best times to get ready for under-ice trapping. When trapping seasons open in February or March there can be four feet of snow on the ice. It is difficult under these conditions to determine the best spot for an under-ice set. The easiest route is to put a dry pole in place in early winter when the snow is light and the ice safe to walk on but not a hassle to cut. At this time it is still easy to see limbs from the beaver's feed pile projecting through the ice. A pole set in position near this feed pile, and later baited with freshly cut aspen, or the favorite beaver food in your area, will produce results if the trap is set on a platform built of small dry limbs nailed to the dry pole. This set works best if the pole is set at a slight slant. Be sure to use a dry pole because a fresh, green pole might be cut and added to the feed pile by an enthusiastic beaver. Bait is wired to the pole just above the trap and just below the ice. To avoid catching young beaver with little market value it is recommended that sets are made some distance from the lodge or feed

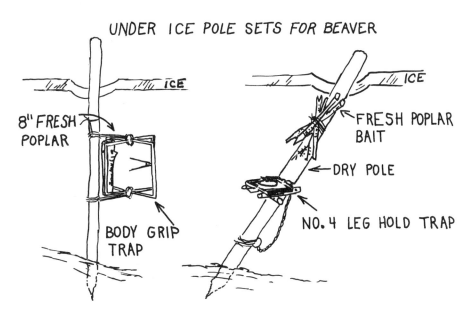

UNDER ICE POLE SETS FOR BEAVER

pile. Young beaver stay close to home. The position of sets for adult beaver can only be determined by the trapper and the situation found at the trapping site. Adult beaver have regular travel routes under the ice. If the ice is clear, look for trails of mud and silt, pieces of bark and grass and other signs of a beaver's travel route under the ice.

The No. 330 size Victor Conibear trap is popular with beaver trappers and can be used with under-ice sets as shown in the illustration. The No. 330 and similar body-grip traps are also used without bait and set between the beaver's lodge and feed pile. It is easy to determine a beaver's route between lodge and feed pile by the trail of twigs and feed. If the water is not deep, one or two body-grip traps will do the job. They should be anchored to stout, dry poles.

Scent Mound Set

In the spring, free-ranging beaver begin posting their area with "scent mounds." These are hamburger size paddies of mud and vegetation that the beaver forms and then anoints with sweet smelling castor emitted from the cloaca. This alerts a wandering adult beaver that a suitable mate may be waiting nearby. To the trapper it means an excellent location for a trap. These scent mounds take on a variety of shapes and substance. Some mounds consist mostly of black river muck and a little grass and are left plastered on icy ledges and snow-covered banks in the early season after the beaver first clears a circular spot in the snow with its tail. Later in the season when the beaver are crawling out onto grassy banks, the scent mounds become less conspicuous as the substance used is mostly vegetation which blends with the surrounding grass and swale. While inconspicuous to the eye, these are excellent set locations. In each instance the trapper must decide the best place to set a trap or traps.

When natural scent mounds are not found, trappers will sometimes make artificial scent mounds from grass and mud and then use a commercial beaver lure to scent the artificial mound. Leg-hold traps can be set in approximately four inches of water for a front leg catch, or a foot of water for a hind leg catch—a favorite with some trappers.

Runway Set

Along any beaver pond or riverside where beaver are active, you can find runways cut into the shoreline. These are formed by the beaver's body when it crawls out of the water to reach areas on the bank that have a lot of favorite foods. The beaver also digs long water channels to reach more distant stands of poplar, cottonwood, willow, or alder. It uses the channels, too, to float tree cuttings to the home pond or riverside. These runways and narrow channels are excellent spots to set a body-grip trap as shown in the illustration. Note that the pole (about 3" in diameter)

RUNWAY SET FOR BEAVER

←POPLAR BAIT

SCENT MOUND

ONE WAY GUIDE

SCENT MOUND SET FOR BEAVER

←DROWNING WIRE

holding the body-grip trap acts as an obstacle to a swimming beaver and induces it to dive under the pole and into the trap.

Beaver do abandon some runways, so you'll want to look for signs of recent activity like tracks, or bank trails wet and muddy from recent use, and fresh cuttings nearby. If you've doubts about the freshness of a runway, you can enhance its appeal to a passing beaver by adding freshly cut bait sticks of poplar and by using lure.

A blind set is a trap placed where you believe a beaver will step on it. Different combinations of types of trap and location are better than others. In some cases the steel leg-hold trap is best; in a varying situation the body-grip trap is more effective. When the water is deep enough to submerge a body-grip trap in a narrow beaver passageway, you have a set that is hard to beat. That narrow passageway may be a break in the center of an old beaver dam. Sometimes it's a road culvert that bisects a beaver colony. The trap should be set with the top of the trap just under the surface of the water as shown in the runway set illustration. The pole holding the trap should rest within an inch of the water, inducing the beaver to dive under the pole and into the waiting trap. You can narrow a passageway by using guide sticks.

When using the steel leg-hold trap at a runway or near a scent mound set, the trap chain should be connected to a drowning wire, as illustrated. Or instead you may stake the trap solidly in deep water with a long extension chain or wire and tie a heavy (5 lb.) sack of rocks or similar weight a foot or so below the trap. This will serve to tire a trapped beaver and soon drown it.

Because they weigh little, snares are used by some trappers when they must hike long distances to reach beaver ponds. A snare is set much the same as a body-grip trap with a pole wedged across the surface of the water in a narrow passageway or channel, inducing the beaver to dive under the pole and into the waiting loop, or loops, of wire. Painstaking trappers sometimes hang a number of snares to increase their chances of a catch. Loops are generally made about 10″ in diameter, 8″ for small beaver. They are also used in under-ice sets by hanging them through a hole cut in the ice between a beaver's lodge and feed pile. When a good quality self-locking snare such as those manufactured by Raymond Thompson is used, a snared beaver rarely escapes.

Beaver are skinned "open" and the pelt is nailed to a flat board in a round or oval shape. You'll find details on skinning beaver in Chapter 7. After you read how to skin, flesh and dry a beaver pelt, it's still a good idea to watch the job done by a professional skinner at a fur buying house or by an experienced trapper. Without the proper tools and know-how, it can be a miserable job. Many a trapper brings his beaver to a fur buyer to be skinned and fleshed for $2 or $3 apiece.

OTTER

A sleek, elongated member of the weasel family, completely adapted to living in water and seemingly enjoying it more than any other animal, the river otter is good-natured dynamite. For all its playfulness, the otter is a

J. E. Osman   *(Courtesy, Pa. Game Commission)*

ferocious fighter with a powerful bite. The otter in a steel trap is a twisting bundle of undulating muscle and fury. If the trap was set for mink or muskrat, the otter is free in seconds. Only large traps such as those suitable for beaver will hold this streamlined bearer of one of the most beautiful and durable of furs. It is just as well that it easily escapes from small traps because the otter is fully protected in many areas and only limited trapping is allowed in others. Considered a difficult animal to trap, it is probably more the case that they are relatively few and their home range large, sometimes covering fifty to a hundred miles of shoreline. Where plentiful, they are no more difficult to trap than mink.

Overall body length for otter—which can include a heavy tail up to 18″ in length—is 35″–55″. Weight varies from 10–30 lbs. Fur color ranges from dark brown to nearly black with grey belly fur. The eyes are near the top of the head to facilitate the otter's seeing while cruising along almost totally submerged. The feet are webbed. Frequently seen undulating through the water like a dolphin, or swimming powerfully underwater, the otter comes up for air five to seven times to the mile.

Otter are found in limited numbers throughout most of the North American continent. Many are trapped in Louisiana, which state takes the greatest number of muskrat. Breeding is in late winter and a litter of one to five are born (in a secluded den, frequently under a river bank) from January to May, after ten to thirteen months, because of delayed implantation. Mating is usually right after young are born.

Otter are always found near water although they can travel easily overland in a distinctive loping gait. They have a keen sense of smell, and are famous for their ability to catch even the swiftest of trout. Included in their diet are fish of all kinds, frogs, clams, crayfish, snakes, turtles, and small animals. The otter seems to have a dislike for mink and will kill a mink on contact. Look for otter in wild areas containing many interconnecting streams, rivers, lakes, and ponds. In some areas, trapping seasons coincide with those for beaver.

The Slide Set

The otter has a passion for steep banks. In the summer a family of otter will wet a mud bank down with their soaking fur and slide again and again until the slide is slick enough to send them into the water at great speeds. They will do the same on a bank of ice and snow. These are excellent set locations. Because the otter slides with the front feet tucked under its belly, a leg-hold trap is not the best for use at the base of a slide. Also the water depth may be too great. It is best to set one or two traps where the otter climbs out of the water to have another try at the slide. The trapper with body-grip traps of a size suitable for beaver might consider submerging a body-grip trap where the otter are splashing into the water at the base of the slide. Indians commonly used snares at otter slides. Because otter travel at times in pairs and even whole families, it is a good idea to set two or even three traps at a good set location such as the one just described. A double catch can be made.

Baited Log Set

A log projecting out of the water is a good location to lure otter with a fresh fish bait. The fish, a foot-long sucker for example, can be nailed to the log just above the water line. The trap is set on the log under six inches of water and wired to the underwater end of the log. Take deliberate care when anchoring traps set for otter. Every effort should be made to drown them quickly; otherwise, this powerful animal may escape.

Beaver Dam Set

Most streams where otter are found also have beaver—and old beaver dams. When these dams start giving way it is usually in the center. For an otter traveling the waterway this is a natural spot to swim. If there is a slight drop in water level it will appeal to the otter's sense of playfulness. If the water is four to six inches deep above the dam, a leg-hold trap can

SLIDE SET
FOR OTTER

TRAP SET
WHERE OTTER
LEAVES WATER →

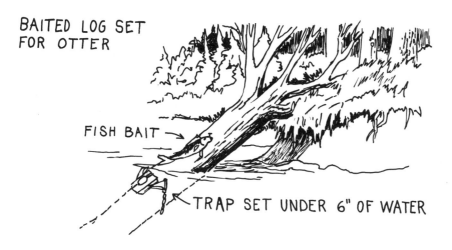

BAITED LOG SET
FOR OTTER

FISH BAIT →

←TRAP SET UNDER 6" OF WATER

be used and will catch the otter by a hind leg, since the front feet are commonly tucked in when swimming. The body-grip trap can be used effectively if the water is too deep for the leg-hold trap. This set will also take traveling beaver.

Many blind sets will take otter. Like the mink, otter will take overland shortcuts across sharp bends in rivers and streams. A good sized animal, the trail they leave in traveling overland is easily seen. Look for tracks in

BEAVER DAM SET FOR OTTER

TRAP SET IN OPENING OF OLD DAM

mud and sand where they are entering and exiting the water. If a log is lying submerged under a few inches of water in midstream, an otter will commonly travel the length of it. One or two leg-hold traps will take it. Beaver ponds are favorite hangouts for otter. In fact, in most northern areas otter are caught when trappers are actually after beaver. After freeze-up, look for spring holes, rapids, or other openings in the ice where otter are entering and exiting the water. Look for tracks in the snow. Sometimes, when traveling overland in ice and snow, an otter will build up speed, fold its front legs up out of the way, and slide on its belly.

Don't overlook the fact that otter can be lured with bait. In addition to the baited log set, you can anchor a fish, guarded by traps, in a shallow riffle. Simply run a wire through the fish's mouth and out the anus. The two ends of wire can be tied to a log lying beside and parallel with the fish. The log also serves as an anchor for the traps. You can put bait in natural rock cubbies or under overhanging tree roots—the possibilities are endless.

Steel leg-hold traps for otter should be No. 4 in underspring or double longspring. Body-grip traps should be comparable to the Victor Conibear 330 size. Whatever trap used, take pains that it is solidly anchored in deep water whenever possible since it will not necessarily kill instantly. Otter are case-skinned and the tail is split and nailed flat. Otter are difficult to skin since a knife must be used to separate the hide from the carcass every inch of the way. The fleshing job is no picnic either. Otter pelts usually bring a high price on the market. Stretching boards should be 50″ long, 9″ wide at the base and 7½″ wide at the shoulder.

SKUNK

The four kinds of skunk in the United States and Canada are: the striped skunk, the hooded skunk, the spotted skunk, and the hog-nosed skunk. And many an older trapper feels a nostalgic pang when a light essence of skunk hangs in the fall air because, like the common muskrat, skunks are one of the first animals trapped by the young trapper. They are prolific, easy to catch, and can be found almost anywhere.

From the 1–2 lb. spotted skunk to a hefty 10 lb. striped, hooded, or hog-nosed skunk, they all can emit—with keen muscular control and in various doses—a vile stream of musk from twin jet nozzles located just inside the anal tract. This they do with fair accuracy to fifteen feet. They are generally loath to use this ultimate weapon and even a trapped skunk

J. E. Osman   (Courtesy, Pa. Game Commission)

will not discharge a spray unless harrassed by a dog or closely approached by the trapper. Their coloration is black with various patterns of white spots or stripes.

The hooded and hog-nosed skunk are pretty well confined to Mexico and the southwestern United States. The striped skunk is found in all of the contiguous forty-eight states and in all provinces of Canada except for the extreme north and Alaska. The spotted skunk is found throughout most of the United States but rarely in Canada. Generally the little spotted skunk has the least market value. The striped skunk has always been the most sought after. At one time skunk pelts sold for a decent price. It could easily happen again. For many years fox pelts were worthless. At the time of this writing they are bringing the highest prices ever. So keep an eye on the wood-pussy market . . . from a safe distance that is.

For all practical purposes, the four kinds of skunk have similar habits and while their diets vary with the terrain, they'll eat almost anything. So even though the common striped skunk is discussed here, the others are similar and can be taken in the same sets.

Striped skunks breed when they're one year old. The young are born after a gestation period of sixty-three days in a dry underground den, hollow log, or any niche or cave. It is not uncommon for a skunk to raise a litter under a lakeside cottage or summer home. The litter varies from one to seven. Skunks are primarily nocturnal but it's not uncommon to see one during daylight hours, particularly late in the afternoon.

The skunk is truly omnivorous: the diet embraces grubs, beetles, insect larvae, snakes, lizards, grasshoppers, crayfish, fish, turtle eggs, ground-nesting bird's eggs, garden crops, domestic chickens and eggs, carrion, fruit, mice, and small animals. While not true hibernators they will den up during cold weather. Frequently this happens only a few weeks after their fur becomes prime for harvesting, around November 1 in the northern areas of the United States. A warm spell in midwinter will mean skunk tracks in the snow, however.

Skunks can be found from suburban backyards to wilderness terrain. Look for them almost anywhere but concentrate on grassy, weed-choked fields, grassy ditches bordering railroad tracks, abandoned farmyards, around old buildings, in ravines and gullies, and along the edges of fields, pastures, marshes, creeks, and ponds. Dumps are good spots.

Cubby Set

The cubby for skunk is built like a miniature shed, one end is left open. It can be constructed of rocks, logs, or a combination of material found at the set location. The cubby should be about 2′ long, the entrance about 12″ in diameter. Toss leaves and dry grass into the back of the cubby to attract mice and other rodents on a skunk's diet. A cubby can be built

CUBBY SET FOR SKUNK

against an abandoned building by simply leaning a few old boards against one wall. A cubby can be quickly made with logs from an old woodpile. This is a good preseason activity for the skunk trapper. A few weeks prior to trapping season bait the cubbies with chicken heads, fish, meat scraps, fish or game entrails—almost anything that will give off an odor. The bait is tossed into the rear of the cubby. With frequent baitings you can have skunk coming regularly and when the season opens a trap can be set in the entrance and good catches made.

The skunk is not trap-shy but a light trap covering of leaves or grass is a wise precaution. The trap can be staked solid or wired to a drag. If there is the possibility of taking raccoon in these sets, and there are few areas where this is not a possibility, then a drag should be used. Trappers may wish to experiment with the body-grip trap such as the Victor Conibear No. 220.

The Baited Circle Set

This set is easy and quick to make and it works. Dump a generous amount of bait on the ground and circle the bait with large rocks, leaving enough space between the rocks for skunks to walk through and traps to be concealed. The advantage of the baited circle set is that more than one skunk can be caught at the set in one night. Three or four traps are used covering all spaces between the rocks and all are wired to separate drags. If the drags are 4′ to 6′ long, a trapped skunk will become entangled in nearby brush and brambles. Cover the bait lightly with dirt or place brush across it to discourage crows and other scavenger birds from getting caught in the traps. By using very large rocks and extending the brush covering over the tops of the rocks you have in effect a cubby with many entrances. A small woods clearing near a dump would be an ideal location for this set.

BAITED CIRCLE SET FOR SKUNK

As any fox trapper can attest, the dirt-hole set, as described in the material on fox trapping, will take skunk. The large trap size and the caution required for fox trapping are not necessary, however. The No. 1½ trap will do for skunk. The dirt-hole set is a good one to keep in mind because it can be quickly made and is a natural for skunk.

This skunk was trapped in a country garbage dump. Raccoon will also visit dumps looking for tidbits.

It is legal to trap skunk in their dens. Skunk dens can be identified by the presence of long black or white hairs at the den entrance or the remains of beetle shells and insect wings scattered about. Droppings will be found. The entrance to a skunk den is rarely as neat and tidy as that of a woodchuck. Generally there is no skunk odor. Set your trap in the entrance with a light covering of dirt, sand, or grass. A large leaf should first be placed over the trap pan to stop sand or dirt from getting under the trap pan and preventing the trap from functioning. Stake the trap solidly so the skunk cannot seek shelter in the den after being caught. Skunk are difficult enough to dispatch of without first having to pull one from its den. A body-grip trap can be used and if the skunk is caught right it can be killed instantly and no odor released, a skunk that is shot or clubbed releases odor. As with all land trapping, there is risk in using the body-grip trap because animals such as cats or dogs that stumble into the set will be killed or maimed and cannot be released unharmed.

For midwinter trapping, set your trap several feet inside a skunk den, then put bait near the entrance. Pile brush and then snow over the entrance so the odor of the bait will permeate down into the den. The odor will awaken a sleeping skunk and when he comes up to investigate the enticing odor he'll step into the waiting trap.

How to dispatch a skunk caught in the leg-hold trap is a very good question. A .22 slug in the brain will not necessarily do the job effectively. The skunk is killed instantly but its last convulsive body movements often send a stream of musk over the trap and, frequently, the skunk himself. There is testimony that a .22 bullet in mid-spine will bring both instant death and paralysis, thereby preventing even convulsive movement. Still, it is a rare skunk trapper who can entirely escape the skunk's ultimate weapon.

Leg-hold traps should be in size No. $1\frac{1}{2}$ in either underspring or longspring models. The skunk is case-skinned with the tail split and nailed flat. The skunk is a fatty animal and all excess fat should be removed with a knife or fleshing tool. Wood stretching boards should be 30" long, $\frac{1}{2}$" thick, 8" wide at the base, 7" at the shoulder. Those for spotted skunk should be 24" long, $5\frac{1}{2}$" wide at the base and 5" at the shoulder.

OPPOSSUM

Br'er Possum's tail is bare, or so it has been said, because a raccoon tricked him into poking it into the fire, and his mouth is wide because he stretched it laughing at a deer that was trying to shake a persimmon tree.

The oppossum is such an unglamorous creature that few trappers will admit to setting a trap for it. Seldom, it would seem, does a 'possum get caught in a trap set for 'possum. Yet three million of these animals are taken annually. Many of them are taken by hunters, and even the hunters rarely admit to hunting oppossum. They are really chasing raccoon. Yet an oppossum pelt will bring more than a muskrat pelt and they are as easily caught. So it is well worth pelting an accidentally captured oppossum and it makes sense to trap it deliberately too. An added benefit is "'possum and taters," a popular dish in many parts of the South.

The overall appearance of the oppossum is shaggy and disheveled. Perhaps it needs a haircut or a shave? Poor 'possum. The overall length is 2–3'. Weight is 4–12 lbs. The fur color is a grizzled grey or off-white. The tail is bare and prehensile, and the female's belly has a pouch.

The Virginia oppossum got started in South America and has been working its way north ever since. It is found throughout the entire eastern United States and as far north as Canada. The oppossum has also been introduced on the West Coast and is now found throughout most of California, as well as parts of Washington and Oregon.

The oppossum will raise one litter a year in the North, but two litters are common in the South. The gestation period is only two weeks, but the young—from five to sixteen—spend many weeks in the mother's pouch with eyes closed. They cling to the mother's nipples, which swell inside their mouths and provide a constant food supply. Since the female oppossum has thirteen nipples this is the most that can survive in a litter.

The oppossum's diet seems to include anything: worms, bugs, insects of all kinds, carrion, birds' eggs, snakes, lizards, small birds and animals, wild fruit, and a special preference for persimmons. Look for oppossum in farmland interspersed with woodlots and brushy fencerows, and along creeks and ponds.

The Den Set

Oppossum dens may be old woodchuck burrows, log piles, rock piles, hollow trees and logs or almost any natural cave or sheltered nook. You can determine if such a spot is being used by oppossum by their tracks in sand or light soil. The oppossum's hind foot leaves a distinctive print, it is the only North American animal with a grasping thumb. Tracks and trails leading to and from a den are common. Also look for bits of feathers or fur lying near the entrance or tufts of the oppossum's grizzled-grey fur on surrounding brush and briars. Once you have determined that an oppossum is using the den, a leg-hold or body-grip trap can be set in the entrance. You can sometimes take half-a-dozen oppossum from one den. Leg-hold traps should be lightly covered and staked solid.

Oppossum can be taken in baited sets. The bait can either be placed in the back of a natural crevice or hollow log, or a cubby can be built of rocks or logs and the bait placed in back and a trap in the entrance. The entrance to the cubby should be at least 6" to 7" in diameter and the cubby 18" to 24" in length. Bait can be just about anything edible for a not-so-fussy animal. Persimmons are good bait, so are flesh and chicken entrails. Smoked fish is good, it can be smelled for a long distance.

(Courtesy, Pete Czura)

DEN SET FOR OPPOSSUM

The dirt-hole set will take oppossum just as it will a wide variety of other animals and can be constructed as described in the section on fox trapping, however the precautions needed for the sly fox are not necessary for oppossum. A No. $1\frac{1}{2}$ size leg-hold trap will hold oppossum.

The oppossum is case-skinned. Like that of the muskrat, the pelt does not have a tail. Unlike the muskrat it is very fatty, all excess fat should be removed. The hide tends to be oily on oppossum and occasionally it should be wiped off with a piece of burlap or other coarse material until it finally dries. Stretching boards for oppossum should be 30″ in length, $\frac{1}{2}$″ thick, and 8″ wide at the base, 7″ at the shoulder.

FOX

For some, fox trapping is what trapping is all about. Either the red fox or the grey fox, sometimes both, can be found on almost every trapline. The red fox in particular is available to trappers all across North America. Shy, cautious from birth, and with inherent cunning, it has good eyesight, acute hearing, and an excellent sense of smell. While the red fox has the edge in being the most difficult to lure into a trap, both the red and the grey fox are a challenge and a delight to the trapper. This chapter is an indepth study of the characteristics of foxes and the best methods to trap them.

The red fox is about the size of a small dog. The fur is bright yellowish-red above, white underneath, with blackish lower legs and feet. Ears are pointed and stand erect. The silver, cross, black, and other colors are phases of the red coat and have the characteristics noted. The red fox weighs from 9–16 lbs.

The grey fox is grey with orange, black, and white markings. It weighs from 4–13 lbs. The grey fox is one up on the red fox: the former can climb trees. However, only the red fox has the protective tufts of fur between the feet pads. This is probably an advantage in ice and snow.

The red fox is the most widespread of the foxes. With the exception of parts of the extreme Southeast, Southwest, and the Plains states, it is found throughout most of North America. The grey fox is found in the Southwest and throughout all of the entire eastern United States and fills in some of the gaps where the red fox is not found.

Other fox found are the little kit fox, in the Southwest and the Plains along the eastern edge of the Rockies, and the arctic fox, found in the extreme northern reaches of Alaska and Canada.

Red fox licking snow

Fox mate in January or February and an average of four to six young are born in the spring, in an underground den—frequently an old woodchuck burrow that has been enlarged. Hollow logs, rock piles, and other natural enclosures are sometimes used, particularly by the grey fox.

The red fox prefers the more open farmlands while the grey fox is at home in heavier undergrowth of briar thickets and scrub oaks, as well as laurel and rhododendron swamps. Some areas will hold equal numbers of both red and grey foxes. In other parts, the grey is confined to a few areas of heavy growth while the red predominates on the more open farmland. In areas where the cover is more suitable to grey fox, he may drive out any red foxes in the area. Red fox are afraid of the scrappy grey fox.

Bobcats, lynx, mountain lions, wolves and coyotes will kill foxes. In the wooded terrain of the North, which is frequented by larger predators, the red fox usually avoids deep woods, finding it more productive—and safer—to hunt the edges of forests. Both the red and the grey will eat a variety of foods; favorites are mice, rats, rabbits, small birds, eggs, snakes, lizards, insects, wild fruit, carrion, as well as farmyard chickens, ducks, and eggs.

In the winter months, fox become far more carnivorous, hunting mice, rabbit, pheasant, partridge, and quail. They will dig through two feet of snow for some tidbit of carrion. At this time they are very susceptible to bait and lure but keeping traps in working order is difficult.

The long auto trapline is popular for fox trapping. Sets are adequate over a knoll from the road—out of sight of passing cars—as long as they are near travel routes used by fox. A single trapper has caught as many as 500 to 600 red fox between late summer and early winter. Such big catches were made when fox pelts were worth only a $5–$6 bounty.

During the 1974–75 season, trappers were paid $35 to $65 for top quality red fox pelts. Needless to say, interest in trapping fox is high. However, as fox become scarce in an area, fewer trappers pursue them. Fox populations bounce back in a hurry. The red fox is unprotected by seasons in most states and some hunters and trappers would like to see restrictions imposed. This would curtail den digging and early season trapping when immature fox, whose fur is not prime, are caught and end late season trapping when fox furs are rubbed (with long guard-hairs broken off) and in poor condition. Throughout the northern states, November, December, and January are the best months for prime, top quality red fox pelts, and even in January some fox pelts will be rubbed and not at their best. Pelts are prime in the southern states from December through February.

Lures and Baits

If trapping in an area where both red and grey fox are found, remember that red fox are afraid of grey fox. It is wise when using urine with fox sets to use red fox urine. This puts the red at ease yet does not deter the grey from investigating and stepping into a waiting trap.

Trappers' supply houses offer everything the fox trapper will need including bait and a vast array of lures (scent and urine). These include gland lure, sometimes referred to as passion lure; the principal ingredients are the sexual organs, anus, and urine from the female fox while in heat. Food or curiosity lures combine odors that appeal to the wild canines for unknown reasons. Trappers have been mixing together horrible concoctions for years with surprising results. Commercial lures take the guesswork out of the whole messy business. Most, when combined with a good set, will do the job.

Tainted bait, as described in Chapter 4, is very effective for trapping fox. Commercial baits are also very good and less of a nuisance for the urban trapper. These too are tainted and sometimes have extra ingredients for extra appeal. But most trappers like to make their own and homemade tainted bait will do the job.

At this time, commercial lures cost $2 to $2.50 an ounce and as many as twenty-five fox may be taken with the ingredients from an ounce of good lure. When buying lure for the first time, test that from several manufacturers to find which works best for you on your trapline. Sometimes the best of lures is a flop because it is sold at local sporting goods stores and used by amateurs who proceed to educate local foxes to that lure by making poor sets with traps reeking with foreign odor.

Fox urine is an ingredient found in almost every fox lure, but fox urine is also sold separately and is a real must on the trapline. It can be liberally sprinkled at a set location; urine is a wonderful suspicion remover. Trappers commonly rub red fox urine into the gloves they wear for trap setting and will spray it onto the soles of their boots. It is also advisable to spray it near where you have approached a set location. Some urine can be obtained from the carcasses of trapped foxes. Trappers' supply houses sell it in 4 oz., 16 oz. and larger containers. A squeeze-type container is handy for the liberal use of urine. A small bottle with a dropper is best for food or gland lure, which is usually measured in drops.

If you are intent on trying your hand at lure making, this recommendation is from *Pennsylvania Trapping and Predator Control Methods*, by the late Paul L. Failor of the Pennsylvania Game Commission (Failor, incidentally, strongly advises the use of commercial lures):

> One of the first and most simple steps in making a lure is to combine the urine and glands (generally anus) of the animal for which the lure is intended. After this mixture has stood for several weeks it may be used as is or other items may be added. In removing the anus, cut around the vent with a sharp knife and take an inch or two of colon. The rim of the vent may be cut at several places to allow the gland to "bleed."
>
> To make a fox lure, take one pint of quality red fox urine and add five or six anus or rectal glands and the smashed livers and galls from three foxes. Add a few sets of

muskrat musk glands, the number depending on their size or the equivalent amount of beaver castor. Let the mixture stand for one month. If you wish, an ounce of strained honey or fish oil may be added to half of the above mixture, giving you two different lures. For winter trapping add glycerine or mineral oil (four ounces to the pint) and some skunk essence. Skunk essence is a very important ingredient in a cold weather lure; however, your lure should not be overloaded with it. Insert a pointed stick into the scent glands of a dead skunk and stir your mixture with the stick.

Repeat until the proper blend is achieved. Keep a flat piece of glass over the mouth of the jar in which your mixture is ageing to prevent the flies from getting in and at the same time permitting the gases to escape. Stir occasionally and after several months strain off the liquid and place in small bottles. After the caps have been tightened, the cap and neck of the bottle may be dipped in hot paraffin. If the lure is to be kept for a year or more, this will insure against spoilage.

Traps and Equipment

Popular traps for fox are the No. 2 Victor coilspring and the No. 2 Blake & Lamb coilspring. A No. 2 underspring (jump) trap is probably just as adequate. Occasionally the No. 3 underspring trap is used for trapping in ice and snow. These will sometimes break through a light crust of frozen dirt when a smaller trap will not. It is imperative that traps be free of foreign odor. See Chapter 2 for complete details on preparing traps for fox. The body-grip trap is generally considered inadequate for fox.

In addition to deodorized traps, the fox trapper must have a dirt sifter with $\frac{1}{4}''$ mesh screen. These can be bought but it is easy to make your own. Build a frame of four pieces of $10''$ long, $2''$ wide, and $\frac{1}{2}''$ thick hardwood. Staple the $\frac{1}{4}''$ mesh screen to the frame. Use $4\frac{1}{2}'' \times 7''$ wax paper or light canvas cloth for trap covering. To complete the job, you'll need a small shovel and/or a hand trowel, a hand cultivator or scratcher, a hand axe, a clean pair of canvas or rubber gloves, and a packbasket or backpack.

The Dirt-Hole Set

The dirt-hole set is, without doubt, the most famous for taking fox and other animals including wolf, coyote, bobcat, raccoon, skunk, oppossum, mink, and weasel. The value of the dirt-hole set is that fox and coyote in particular have a habit of digging holes to bury food they want to eat at a later date. The trapper attempts to imitate such a dug hole and then adds bait, scent, and urine. To the fox it will appear that another fox has buried some food—what better than to steal this easy meal? But the would-be thief is worried, scared. What if the fox that buried the bait is lurking nearby or . . . heaven forbid . . . a human?

Placement of the dirt-hole set is all-important. It should be kept out in the open, away from high grass, trees, large rocks, and stumps. An unused

DIRT HOLE SET FOR FOX

pasture or field of stubble and a nearby woodland or marsh hunted by fox is ideal. The set should be at least fifty feet from the edge of the marsh or woods and an equal distance from anything else the fox cannot see over. This will put the fox at ease and allow it to feel in control of the situation while approaching what looks and smells like a tasty meal. If you have done your part well, the fox will not know how wrong it is until the trap snaps shut.

Open fields with short grass are not always easy to find in heavily forested country, but the principle can still be applied. Follow old logging trails and roads that bisect forested areas and select a set location within thirty feet of the trail that is fairly open, free of high weeds and undergrowth. Pick a spot for the set where the fox can see at least twenty feet around the set. A good idea, at any set location, is to dig the dirt hole at an angle under a low rock, rotten log, or tuft of grass, but be sure the backing is low enough for the fox to see over the top easily. The backing is to discourage an investigating fox from approaching the bait and hole from the side opposite where the trap is set.

It is invaluable to know the travel and hunting routes of fox. An easy way to discover some of them is to get out in the winter months and see where fox tracks are crossing dirt roads and highways. The best fox trapper the author has ever met first hunted fox with hounds for many years before he began trapping them. He knew where fox traveled in numerous areas in the county where he lived. It was only natural to select open fields and clearings near these travel routes for his dirt-hole sets.

The making of the dirt-hole set is simple. Wear clean canvas or rubber gloves and rubber footwear. With a small shovel or hand trowel cut a triangular clump of sod about one foot from corner to corner. The corner where the dirt-hole is to be dug should be against a low rock or other backing. The sod removed should be 2″ to 3″ thick. Shake some of the excess dirt from the sod into the excavated area. Toss the sod as far as you

The dirt-hole set ready for action. Small stone acts as backing to discourage fox from digging into the back of the hole. Bait and lure are used.

can into nearby high grass or carry it away with you after completing the set. Next dig a hole about 3″ in diameter and 6″ deep in the corner and at a 45° angle under the backing. Scatter this dirt just as far as you can throw it. Next dig a trap bed directly in front of the hole so one jaw of the trap will be about 1″ from the edge of the hole. The trap bed should be deep enough so that the set trap will be slightly below the level of the surrounding dirt. Put this dirt into your sifter.

Before setting the trap in place, drive a stake into the trap bed. The stake should be 12″ long for clay soil, longer for sand. The trap chain is wired to the trap stake by the fourth link from the trap. With the chain so shortened, a trapped fox will not be able to make high leaps and possibly pull loose. Pound the stake completely into the ground, slightly below the level of the trap bed. Now take your $4\frac{1}{2}$″ x 7″ wax paper—crumple it first to prevent it from rattling—tear a slit for the trap dog (trigger mechanism) and then place it over the trap pan with the ends under the trap jaws. Set the trap firmly in the trap bed with the trap dog toward the hole. The excess trap chain is tucked under the trap. The trap should set solidly and not rock should a fox first step on a jaw before encountering the trap pan. Now take your dirt sifter and sift the dirt in it over your trap to a depth of about $\frac{1}{4}$″. Your trap pan should be set on a hair-trigger and slightly below the level of the jaws. When covering the trap with sifted dirt, the area of the pan should still be slightly below the level of the jaws and surrounding dirt. Fox are inclined to place their feet in such a low spot when sniffing the hole. With your scratcher, level out the dirt over the set area, blending some of the dirt into the surrounding grass.

A chunk of bait can now be placed in the hole. A stiff piece of wire works well for spearing a piece of bait from the bait jar. Drop the bait into the hole, being careful not to spill juice on the buried trap. This could cause the fox to dig where the trap is, which usually results in a sprung trap rather than a trapped fox. Pour a few drops of good gland lure on the edge of the hole, letting it run down in. With the scratcher straighten up the grass where you have been crouching and sprinkle this area and the trap bed with red fox urine. That's it. This set will take any fox that comes along.

Most sets improve with age but the expert trapper likes to make a catch the first night. The best way to get overnight success with the dirt-hole set is to make the set quickly and with a minimum of fuss. The way to accomplish this is to do the sod cutting part of the dirt-hole set several weeks in advance of setting the trap. This in itself will attract fox. The smell of fresh dirt is attractive to fox as it is to dogs and other canines who dearly love to dig a hole. By the time you are ready to set the trap there will probably be fox tracks at the set location. With sod already removed you should be able to complete this set in minutes. Avoid kneeling on the ground as this will leave human odor. Crouch down on your heels.

Even without the sod removed ahead of time, the pros can make a dirt-hole set in just minutes and make a catch the first night. What it takes is practice. If you have never used this set before, by all means practice making it in your backyard or nearby field. Selection of a good set location and speedy trap setting is what pays off in fox trapping.

There will be little sod to remove if you can find a sandy spot. Some spots are simply too rocky or interwoven with roots to make a good dirt-hole set. Know the problems ahead of time.

Other animals will be attracted to your dirt-hole sets. In the East, the oppossum is a dreaded catch. The odor of oppossum at a set location or on a trap is distasteful to fox. Rather than use this set again, trappers will make another set nearby using a clean trap. The trap that caught the oppossum must be thoroughly cleaned before it can be reused.

Skunk and raccoon are the other two principal animals that will mosey into a dirt-hole set. Neither will ruin the set; in fact, a little essence of skunk may improve it. If the skunk has released a lot of musk when it was dispatched of (usually skunk are shot in the spine or chest area with a .22 caliber weapon), leave the skunk in the trap until the air has a chance to clear. This will take a day or so. The skunk is then removed and the trap reset. The only problem is if a lot of blood gets on the trap or surrounding dirt when a skunk or raccoon is shot. This does not frighten fox; to them it is food smell; the problem is they tend to dig the trap up. So if a trap gets bloody, set a clean one and also scoop away any dirt soaked with blood.

When a fox has been caught in a dirt-hole set, the set is improved. It is true that your neatly constructed set will now be messed up, but the odor left by the trapped fox is a super scent for luring more fox. Simply spruce up the set, dig out the dirt hole if it has been plugged, and rebait. Usually lure is added about every three days. This is not necessary if a fox has been caught and scented down the set.

The dirt-hole set can be used after freezing and even deep snow if the dirt can be kept dry. Dry dirt can be stored in pails in a shed or other clean, airy spot for use in winter trapping. Dry dirt will not freeze. Antifreeze solutions can be bought, usually with fox urine added, and sprayed on a set to prevent freezing. Some believe that fox shy from a set so treated, others find it rusts their traps, a few trappers are well satisfied with the results.

A word about killing a trapped fox. The best way to do it is to stun the fox by rapping it across the nose with the handle of the shovel used in making sets. Then pin the animal's neck to the ground with the grip end of the shovel and kneel or step on the side of the fox's chest. With the lungs collapsed, death comes within seconds. This prevents blood at the set, the fur is not damaged, and it is as humane as any method.

Red fox like this one can be taken in the dirt-hole set even after snow blankets the ground.

Scent-Post Set

Just as the domestic dog will raise its leg and direct a stream of urine where another dog has urinated, fox will do the same when detecting the odor of fox urine on a tuft of grass or piece of dry wood planted in the ground by the trapper. The grass, absorbent dry wood, or low bush can be natural or planted but should not measure over 3″–5″. Scenting posts chosen by fox are usually objects standing alone along the trail. This set should be made along the foxes' travel route. By setting two traps, one on either side of the scent post, double catches can be made in one night provided the traps are attached to individual drags or toggles. If the set is made in open country near a fenceline, for example, traps should be staked solid. Drags work best when traps are set along woods trails; here the trapped fox cannot get far before hanging up.

A good set location is in the middle of an old tire-track trail winding through a woods. The male fox can raise his leg and the female fox can

81

SCENT POST SET FOR FOX

SCENT

straddle the post. The natural or planted scent post can be scented a week or two before setting traps. Use at least half an ounce of red fox urine to a set. Follow the same exacting precautions needed for the dirt-hole set. This set will fool those fox who have become wise to the dirt-hole set.

Mound Set

If you have ever seen a fox approach a large bait such as a dead deer, cow, sheep, pile of meat scraps or entrails, you will know that it does so with considerable caution. It will circle the bait again and again for

MOUND SET FOR FOX

several nights and leap onto stumps or mounds of earth for a more advantageous look. Finally it will gather the nerve to risk that valuable skin. Even after the animal has settled down to nightly feeding on the bait, it will circle and hop onto high spots each night before dining. These high spots are where you set your traps. An ant hill is ideal. It is easy to conceal a trap and then return the ant hill to its original appearance. Stump tops are good if the surface is rotted and contains fine material for trap covering. If you are setting out the bait yourself, select a good set location that also has good trap-setting locations. In the case of found carrion, you will have to make do with what is available in the way of trap-setting locations. Sometimes the carrion can be moved to a better spot.

This set has the added advantage of being "pet proof," a stray or free-ranging cat or dog will head straight into the bait. No lure or urine is used with the mound set. Use clean traps and wear clean canvas or rubber gloves. If cover is nearby, wire a drag or toggle to each trap. Several traps can be used if enough suitable mounds or stumps are found.

Campfire Set

It is common knowledge that skunk, raccoon, and black bear frequent campgrounds, moseying in after dark and foraging for goodies. Fox and coyote, however, are also aware of these sources of free meals. After the camping season is over and a hint of winter is in the air, a campground is

CAMPFIRE SET FOR FOX

a good location for the campfire set although a secluded campsite can be effective even during the camping season. Fox will come into camp-grounds and other common camping sites at night and search for scraps, some of the tastiest are found in the ashes of campfires. Burned tidbits of bacon and gristle are like dessert to a hungry fox.

Select a campground that is far from farms and ranches and the resulting cats and dogs. Locate an old campfire and clear a hole in the ashes about 4″ deep and 15″ across; place the ashes on a piece of canvas or in a paper bag. Set two No. 2 or No. 3 size traps in the excavated space, solidly anchored with a stake driven out of sight below the traps. Now sift approximately ½″ of ash over the traps and cleared space. If the ashes are light and the traps set on hair-triggers, trap covers are not needed. Carry away the excess ashes and scatter them a good distance from the set.

To make this set even more effective, burn a small bundle of dry grass over the completed set. Add a few pieces of bacon rind, meat scraps, or cracklings to the fire. Several chicken feathers added to the fire will produce a strong and—to the fox—enticing smell. You can also put fox lure on a nearby tree. Placed overhead, the scent will be broadcast farther and lure more fox.

The Snare Set

When the snow is a foot or more deep, the leg-hold trap is a poor choice for fox trapping except in the hands of the most expert trappers and even for the experts it is frustrating and difficult to keep leg-hold traps in working order. One solution is the self-locking steel snare. The principal manufacturer is Raymond Thompson of Lynnwood, Washing-ton. The U.S. Air Force has been a customer of Thompson's since 1948, and the Air Force survival kit includes the smaller snares for catching muskrat, mink, or rabbit.

Snaring is most effective when soft, deep snow induces fox and other animals to stick to established trails. Generally, snares are only legal in wild terrain where there is little chance of catching dogs or cats. In some instances, the trapper must obtain a permit from the local conservation officer in the area he plans to set snares. He may be further advised of restrictions on the size of the snare noose and the illegality of setting snare in deer trails. Restrictions on the use of the steel snare will vary with the state or province. Always check with your local game enforcement office, details of these and other restrictions will not always appear in the general hunting and trapping regulations of your state or province.

Some trappers will whitewash their snares to blend with the snow; others prefer to blacken their snares, as they would the leg-hold trap, so that they blend with branches and undergrowth. Still others believe

SNARE SET FOR FOX

there is no need for any special treatment. The author has successfully used untreated snares. It is surprising to trappers who have never used them but snares—although exposed to view—are not noticed by fox if free of odor and set in heavy cover. To the fox it is another vine or twisted briar branch to which it pays scant attention. If kept in an airy shed, snares will stay fairly odor-free. The cold weather of midwinter also helps to curtail foreign odors. The trapper should wear clean canvas gloves when setting snares, however.

Fox tracks in the snow are your guide to where to make snare sets. Avoid setting snares in sparse, open country, where they could be obvious. Find where fox are hunting or traveling through willow swamps or the thick cover of secondgrowth poplar following fire or logging. Evergreen thickets are good. Walk a trail through thick evergreens and where fox tracks cross the trail snares can be set amid pine boughs on either side of the trail. A favorite set location is where fox are moving from one thicket or island of trees to another, passing through high grass and swale enroute. Fox may scamper all through a thicket of trees and brush but when moving on to the next patch of cover they use the same trail. Trails through high grass and swale are often tunnel-like and ideal for a snare set.

A fox trail is often a single set of tracks, for the animal places its feet in the same tracks each time. Even the winding helter-skelter tracks obviously made by hunting fox will often be followed step by step by the same fox the next time it returns. It will be a week or more before the fox returns, so leave a snare hanging at least that long in any one spot.

When making the snare set, first place a sapling (3″–4″ in diameter) across the trail and about a foot above the trail, unless you have found a natural setup where fox are slipping through a small opening under a limb or windfall. Hang the snare noose directly below the pole. In high grass or swale where there are no trees, you can attach the end of the snare to the pole which acts as a drag. The pole forces the fox to lower its head into the snare. A pole above the snare may also be a legal requirement. Should a deer use the same trail, the pole will act as an obstacle for the deer to step over and prevent the animal's getting a foot caught in the snare. The noose for fox snaring should be 8″ in diameter and the bottom of the noose 4″ above the trail. When snares are set in rabbit trails, which is often the case when fox are hunting rabbits, the rabbits can run under the noose but the larger fox will be caught. In small, natural openings under windfalls and the like where fox are obviously just squeezing through, you may have to have the bottom of the snare noose resting right in the snow.

Use weed stalks or small twigs thrust into the snow to hold the snare noose in place. This also helps to break up the outline of the snare. Light thread can be used to tie the sides of the snare loop to guide sticks. But handling thread gets frustrating with cold-stiffened fingers. Scatter a light coating of snow over the completed set and fill in your footprints for a few feet from the set.

One of the delights of using a snare is that freezing and thawing temperatures will not knock it out of commission. Snowfall, except for really heavy precipitation, only enhances the snare set. The end of the snare should be attached as high above the set as it will reach. Extension wire can be added to a short snare, thus it is easier to locate if buried in deep snow. Favorite snares are those a full six feet in length, but some states impose a three-foot limit, however, the higher a fox can leap after being caught the better are the chances of its becoming entangled off the ground and asphyxiating itself.

With fox pelts selling at premium prices, the competition is fierce for the hobby trapper tackling fox for the first time. But it is by no means impossible to catch them. Fox are smart but man can outmaneuver animal. Time-proven sets like the dirt hole and scent post will fool the smartest fox when made with clean traps and in the right spots.

Fox pelts are dried fur side out. Stretching boards for fox should be 50″ long, 9″ wide at the base, 7½″ wide at the shoulder. After one night on the board flesh side out, the pelt should be turned and the drying process completed with the fur side out.

COYOTE AND WOLF

The coyote and wolf are the two most intelligent animals the trapper is likely to encounter. Trappers who successfully trap coyote and wolf are invariably crack hunters and woodsmen as well as expert trappers. Both canines are similar in habits and sets that will take the one will generally take the other. Timber wolves are much the larger however, and powerful traps are needed to hold them. The hobby trapper who wants to try his hand at this game will have a tough go of it, but even the newcomer to trapping can take these animals if he is willing to work at it and follows the methods described here. Only trappers based in Alaska or Canada are likely to have a chance at trapping the timber wolf, but the coyote—or "brush wolf" as he is called—is available to many and a challenge and an adventure to trap. Do not underestimate this character. Once it's had its toes pinched in a set where bait and scent have been used, it may never approach another, depending entirely on fresh kills.

Timber wolves vary in color from black to white but are usually a grizzled-grey. The largest roam the arctic coasts of Canada, where weights of up to 175 pounds have been recorded. On the average, the timber wolf weighs from 60–125 pounds. The coyote is more uniformly grizzled-grey in color and weighs from 20–50 pounds—essentially, a wolf in a smaller package. According to an Indian legend, it will be the last animal on earth.

The timber wolf still abounds in the Canadian wilderness and in Alaska. In the lower forty-eight states, Minnesota is the last stronghold. While the larger wolf is losing ground, the coyote is forever extending its range and is found in almost every state west of the Mississippi and east of the Mississippi in Wisconsin, Michigan, Illinois, and Indiana. It is reported in

many of the far eastern states and is now established in the Adirondacks. In Canada only the easternmost provinces are free of coyote. It is well established in Alaska although it did not appear there before 1900. The coyote or brushwolf is not only sly, it is a highly adaptable animal—one way or the other, it is here to stay.

Coyotes and wolves breed in winter, usually in January or February. The gestation period is approximately two months, with a litter of three to eighteen young, six or seven is the average. The den may be an enlarged badger burrow, hollow log, or natural cave. The timber wolf likes a rise of ground nearby to use as an observation point. The den of the coyote is characterized by a semicircle of earth around the entrance; this is formed by the animal after it digs the hole.

The wolf is essentially a meat eater and will kill deer, moose, mountain sheep, caribou, musk oxen, elk, pronghorn, rabbits, paririe dogs, mice and other small mammals, and will take domestic stock. The coyote will also take big game animals but more often feeds on the carcasses of large game. Like the fox and wolf, the coyote is always ready to eat carrion. The diet includes a host of other foods—just about anything it can swallow. The eating habits of fox, coyote, and wolf are very similar; the coyote, however, will go after larger prey than the fox, and the wolf will take over where the coyote leaves off. Given the opportunity, a timber wolf will kill a coyote who, in turn, will kill a fox. All will prey to some extent on domestic stock, a habit that puts them in a bad light with farmers and ranchers. They are hunted, trapped, and poisoned, yet these wild canines continue to thrive and—in the case of the fox and the coyote—to prosper. They are not only sly but have a tenacious zest for life. Many tidbits go into the diets of coyote and wolf: snakes, lizards, birds, eggs, grasshoppers and other insects; the coyote has a passion for watermelon.

Because they require large amounts of meat, the timber wolf simply cannot exist in large numbers near farming and ranching country. The temptation of domestic stock, particularly if wild game is scarce, leads them into conflict with man and the annihilation of the wolf. As a result, the timber wolf is more populous in wilderness terrain. The amount of big game animals in an area usually determines the number of wolf that can exist in the area. The smaller coyote or brushwolf is able to live almost anywhere and in some of our western states will even be found within city suburbs. In northern Minnesota, Wisconsin, and Michigan, it is inclined to stick to wild terrain and is less frequently seen in those states than in parts of California, Texas, New Mexico, Arizona, and South Dakota.

In forested terrain look for coyote and wolf sign, tracks and droppings, along old lumber trails and along the edges of small backcountry roads. Look for their sign in clearings around abandoned homesteads and lumber camps. Watch for their tracks in the mud along beaver ponds. Both coyote and wolf will follow river banks.

In the West, look for coyote sign in sandy arroyos—dry gullies. A game trail, such as a deer trail, is also a good place to look for sign. In arid country, a spring or springhole is an ideal place to look for tracks, also trails leading to the spring. Check with sheep ranchers and chicken and turkey farmers and ask if they have seen coyote.

The preparations for coyote and wolf trapping are much the same as those detailed in the material on fox trapping. Traps and other gear must be odor-free. If steel stakes or grapples are used, these must be as odor-free as your traps. Hardwood stakes can be used for coyote trapping if long enough not to pull out of the ground. Some trappers will use a short stake in conjunction with a grapple. The stake, it is hoped, will hold the coyote at the set long enough for the animal to scent-up the set then pull free. The grapple takes over entangling the coyote in the nearest cover. Steel stakes may be available from supply houses but more often are homemade, sometimes fashioned from old steel fenceposts.

Old-hand coyote and wolf trappers tend to like canvas for their trap covers. This should be cut to size then washed and allowed to hang outside for a few weeks. Scents, lures, and baits that will lure fox will also bring in coyote and wolf but when trapping in areas predominated by coyote, for example, you will want to buy specially designed commercial lure. Make tainted bait as described in the material on fox trapping. As with fox trapping, success depends on knowledge of the animal, good set locations, clean traps and accessories, and the wise use of lure and bait.

The Dirt-Hole Set

The dirt-hole set should be made where an approaching coyote or wolf can see in all directions around the set, usually an open meadow or field with sparse vegetation. In the West, a favorite location for the dirt-hole set is an area with many pocket gopher mounds or prairie dog holes. These locations are known to every coyote for miles around. In forested terrain, this set can be made in small clearings near old lumber trails or right along the edge of such a trail. Old homestead clearings are good, even a broad expanse of river sandbar will do the trick.

The dirt-hole set is an imitation of a place where a coyote, wolf, or other animal has cached uneaten food for a later date. Furbearers seem to delight in robbing the food caches of one another, so this set is a favorite with trappers and will take a variety of animals including fox, raccoon, skunk, bobcat, badger, even an occasional mink. The basic design of the set is simply a small dug hole imitating where an animal has buried food. In some instances natural holes can be found in fields frequented by prairie dogs or pocket gophers. An abandoned pocket gopher mound may

DIRT HOLE SET FOR COYOTE AND WOLF

OLD LOGGING TRAIL

DIRT HOLE →

CONCEALED TRAP →

already have a shallow hole in it but if you cannot find one of the proper size, then dig one into the side of a mound. The mound acts as a backing to discourage the animal from approaching the hole from the side opposite to where the trap is set. A small bush, tuft of grass, low rock, or rotten log is good backing for sets made in fields, meadows, and along old logging trails.

If there is sod where you choose to make your set, first cut a triangular piece about fifteen inches from corner to corner. The corner where the hole is to be dug should be up against the backing. In many areas of the West, there is little sod, however, a sandy spot will do. Many coyote and wolf trappers prefer to select sandy spots for their sets rather than add the disturbance of cutting sod. When the 2″–3″ thick sod triangle is removed, shake some of the excess dirt back into the excavated site then toss the sod into nearby high grass or carry it away with you after the set has been completed as it could arouse the animal's suspicion.

Dig the hole approximately 5″ across and 7″–8″ deep, at a 45° angle under the backing. If no sod was removed in making the set, spread the dirt from the hole in a fan-shaped pattern directly in front of the hole. If sod was removed, you already have loose dirt in front of the hole and the dirt from the hole can be tossed as far as possible from the set location. Now dig a trap bed so the trap dog (trigger mechanism) is 2″–3″ from the edge of the hole. The trap bed should be deep enough so that the trap will set slightly below the surrounding dirt. First pound a steel stake into the trap bed, or bury a steel grapple. When staking traps, wire the fourth link of the trap chain nearest the trap to the stake with No. 9 gauge wire; this prevents the animal from leaping high and possibly pulling loose.

The dirt dug from the trap bed should be put in a dirt sifter with $\frac{1}{4}''$ screen and, after the trap is set firmly in place with canvas or wax paper over the trap pan and under the jaws, sifted over the trap to a depth of $\frac{3}{8}''$. With your scratcher or hand trowel, level out the set, blending the dirt with any surrounding grass. The scratch marks will give it a natural appearance. Now put tainted bait into the hole and a few drops of lure on the edge of the hole or on a nearby bush. Coyote or wolf urine can be sprinkled over the set and also where you have worked on the set.

If you're trapping in an area where fox as well as coyote may be caught, it is a good idea to use fox scent and urine at these sets, since coyote will still be attracted and a fox poses no threat to a coyote. Fox, on the other hand, are afraid of coyote.

Carrion Set

Coyote and wolf will feed on carrion such as dead deer, horse, cow, or large bait. The thing to remember when setting traps is that the closer the coyote or wolf gets to the carrion the more suspicious it will be of any disturbance even though it has been feeding nightly. The old hand at coyote and wolf trapping knows this and instead of setting traps right at the bait will make a couple of sets twenty-five yards away.

Dig a trap bed near a low bush or tuft of grass and then, after driving a stake or burying a grapple, set your trap and cover with a light layer of dirt even with the surrounding ground. Sprinkle gland lure or urine on the bush or tuft of grass. Brush out your tracks with a small bush or pine bough. When approaching the bait, the coyote or wolf will notice this

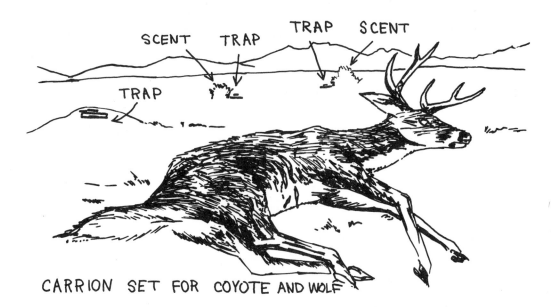

CARRION SET FOR COYOTE AND WOLF

scent and stroll over to investigate, thinking as it does so that another coyote or wolf has been feeding on the free meal ticket—thus it will not be inclined to be suspicious.

Traps can be set on high points of ground without lure as in the mound set for fox. Traps can also be set on trails within a hundred yards of bait. Select a spot in the trail where a trap can be easily concealed. Dig your trap bed right under where the animal has placed a foot. No scent is used with a trail set.

Chaff-Bed Set

This is an excellent set that can be made right in view of the farm or ranch house and still take every predator that comes along. Select a location where the animal will have a good view of the surrounding terrain and where the level of the ground is slightly sloped to allow good drainage, then dump a load of buckwheat chaff about 6' in diameter and 4"–5" deep. Add a few handfuls of grain, plus some cracklings and even some small cubes of peanut butter and cheese. The idea is to lure mice to this spot. This in turn will lure fox, coyote, and wolf. Also scatter hog cracklings and other bait attractive to predators in the surrounding area. When you notice they are digging in the chaff bed, set your traps. Use clean traps with grapples attached. You can set up to four or five traps

The author with a hefty coyote.

THE CHAFF-BED SET FOR COYOTE

and, because the trapped coyote or wolf can leave the set location, it is possible to make more than one catch in a night. Traps can be staked solid if the country is very open and a trapped animal is able to travel a long distance with a grapple before getting entangled in cover.

The Snare Set

The snare set, where legal, is a deadly one for coyote and wolf in forested terrain because their heavy body weight causes them to stick to established trails in snow—this is not the case with the lightweight fox. The wolf has a large range but because snare sets will remain working for long periods under adverse conditions of snow and freezing and thawing temperatures, they have a way of paying off in the long run. Many snare sets can be clustered in hotspots, and when a family or pack of wolves pass through, several animals may be caught. Even without snow the snare set is good. Coyote and wolf leave a lot of sign and it is easy to locate trails even without snow. As a trapper becomes familiar with an area, he will discover trails that are used year after year. A deadly spot for the snare set is on a log where the animals cross a stream or gully.

When setting a snare on a log crossing, find where a limb extends over the log some 20″ above the log or prop a pole above the log at this height and hang a snare noose (10″ in diameter) directly below the pole. The bottom of the noose should be about 10″ above the log. If vines or vegetation of any kind hangs down from overhead limbs, lightly twist them onto the sides of the noose to break up its outline and give it a natural appearance. Thread can be used to tie the sides of the noose to surrounding limbs or to limbs thrust in the snow to narrow the trail and guide the animal into the noose.

In the winter it is common to find where brushwolf or timber wolf are following riverbanks. Find heavy cover through which they travel and set

SNARE SET FOR COYOTE AND WOLF

several snares. Carrion, especially carrion in heavy cover, is a real find for the coyote- and wolf-snaring trapper. Set your snares in the trails leading to the bait and far enough from the bait that the animals are not yet worried about any danger they may encounter at the bait site. Use good quality self-locking snares. The end of the snare wire should be attached to either a standing tree or a heavy drag that the animal cannot chew through and escape.

Fox, wolf, and coyote will sometimes twist or chew a snare beyond reuse. The price of steel snares is considerably less than that of leg-hold traps however, and parts of one snare can be utilized to repair another.

Because coyote and wolf follow regular routes between hunting areas, even before snowfall, the trail set is a popular trap setting. A set that can be made in conjunction with the trail set is the scent-post set which is made like that described in the material on fox. The fact is, fox, coyote, and wolf will all tumble to the same sets. They are all wild canines with much the same habits. Although not illustrated in this material, the scent-post set for coyote and wolf is deadly. Make it just as you would the set for fox except that a slightly higher tuft of grass or bush can be used as the scent post, coyote or wolf urine is used, and the traps should be larger. The scent-post set for any of the wild canines is particularly effective during the breeding season. At this time urine—taken from females in heat—should be used.

Steel leg-hold traps best suited for coyote are the No. 3 or No. 4 size. The underspring or "jump" trap is the most popular for the dirt-hole set because it is easily concealed. Only a top quality, heavy trap will do for wolf trapping. The best made is the Newhouse trap, a double longspring trap of incomparable quality. It is also expensive. Use the No. 4 or No. $4\frac{1}{2}$ size. Coyote and wolf are case-skinned. Wood fur stretchers for coyote should be 5' long, 1' wide at the base and 10" wide at the shoulder. Wolf boards should be 13" at the base and 11" at the shoulder. These boards should be at least $\frac{1}{2}$" thick and sanded smooth. After a pelt has been on the board for several days with the flesh side out, it should be turned and the final drying done with the fur side out.

BOBCAT AND LYNX

Like all cats, these two are built for killing and will range over a lot of country to satisfy their hunger. Bobcat and lynx are populous only in rare instances or in locales where small game and other natural foods are abundant. They demand wild terrain, particularly the lynx, and, while not difficult to trap, will lure the trapper into some pretty rugged country. The greatest difficulty in trapping wildcat is in locating sets where the cats can find them; their sense of smell is poor. At the time of this writing, their pelts are commanding top prices.

The lynx weighs from 12–40 pounds, has long grey fur with flecks of brown and black, tufted ears and a short, black-tipped tail. The bobcat's coat has an almost reddish tone, with dark spots or blotches around the belly and legs—these are more prominent on younger animals. It has a short, white-tipped "bobtail" and weighs from 15–45 pounds. The coat of the bobcat is generally more mottled than that of the lynx. The lynx has much larger feet than the bobcat; in fact, they are oversized but are just the thing for navigating on the surface of the snow, more slender-legged animals flounder in the drifts.

The lynx is found throughout Alaska and Canada and his range blends with that of the bobcat in the northern United States. The bobcat, which is far more able to live near man than the lynx, is found from southern Canada throughout the entire United States and south into Mexico, but is very rare in the Plains states. The lynx, like the wolf, is only able to survive in uninhabited terrain, it prefers heavy forests and is highly dependent on the snowshoe rabbit population, which is its primary source of food.

Both cats breed between January and April and after a gestation period of fifty to sixty days will have an average litter of two to three kittens. These are born in a hollow log, windfall, natural cave, or any suitable den.

The bobcat and lynx live almost entirely on meat. Sometimes they will kill a small deer but more often the quarry is rabbit or other small game animal or bird. The bobcat will occasionally take livestock including sheep, goats, calves, and colts. Lynx will also take livestock but rarely

Bobcat   *(Courtesy, Burnham Brothers)*

come close to human habitation to do so. Both bobcat and lynx have similar habits and the set that will take one will take the other.

In the northern forested regions of the United States and in southern Canada, look for bobcat sign, tracks and droppings, in dense lowlands of spruce and balsam, as well as alder swamps that contain plenty of snowshoe rabbits, ruffed and spruce grouse, and other small game and rodents. In the West, look for bobcat sign along wooded draws and rocky ridges that border or extend into sagebrush flats. In the Southeast, bobcat are found in the deciduous forests with their weedy areas and in swamps. Magnolia climax forests are rich in rodent life and appealing to the bobcat. In the South, bobcat are found in canebrakes and swamps that contain plentiful small animal life. Bobcat seem to flourish in the arid Southwest. Occasionally, it ranges above 6,000 feet but never above 12,000.

Because it must range over great distances to find enough game to keep it alive, particularly during the winter months, the bobcat is hard to locate at any given time or place. But, like other far-ranging animals, it has established routes or circuits, and fresh sign found in the dust or snow of an old logging road or sandy arroyo generally means the cat will return to that spot, perhaps in a few days, perhaps in a few weeks.

The Cubby Set

Bobcat and lynx can be taken in a baited cubby set. Fresh bait is the best but in the winter months the cats are not too fussy, often feeding on the carcasses of long-dead deer and other big game animals. Bait can be a whole rabbit or the entrails and feathers of a grouse. Beaver is an excellent bait, so is muskrat and porcupine. A cubby keeps the bait out of sight of ravens and predatory birds, and it shields the trap from snow and sleet. Toss leaves and grasses into the cubby; this will attract rodents which are in turn preyed upon by the bobcat.

CUBBY SET FOR BOBCAT

An easy cubby to build is one made of poles (dead tree limbs) leaned up against a tree in teepee-fashion; leave an opening in front for one or two traps to be set. Generally, the bait is nailed to the tree.

Dig a bed for the trap or traps and lightly cover the traps with pine needles or leaves. Cats are not trap-shy. The biggest problem is locating cubby sets where the cats can find them. This means plenty of preseason scouting or at least getting out after the snow falls and looking for tracks.

The Bird-Wing Set

The bird-wing set, which could as easily be the rabbit-skin set or hanging-bait set, works on the curiosity of the bobcat. Hang a bird wing, rabbit skin, deer skin, or bait from a tree limb and about five feet above the ground. Pour some good cat lure on the limb. Locate this set where it can be seen for quite a distance. A lone tree not too far from a trail or fringe of timber is a good location. Use a wire to hang the wing, and below the wing build up the ground using dirt or snow, then conceal one or two traps on this mound.

This adaption of the mound set for fox and coyote is obviously for an animal much less trap-shy. The bird-wing set will certainly arouse the curiosity of a fox or coyote but neither is going to risk its neck by coming too close. The bobcat is far less suspicious and a whole lot more curious than either the fox or coyote. This set can actually be improved by hanging a shiny aluminum pie plate by a 3′ length of string from the same tree. This will be seen farther as it dances and sparkles in the wind and sunlight and will incite the bobcat's curiosity. Once near the set it will smell the bait or lure and step into the trap as it leaps onto the handy mound just below the wing. Many trappers feel the bobcat has poor scenting ability and thus strive to add eye appeal to all sets made for the cats.

The dirt-hole set is another good set for bobcat but need not be made in open areas as for fox and coyote. Dig the hole as you would for coyote. Do not cover the bait as is sometimes recommended for fox and coyote; in fact, a little hair or feathers protruding from the dirt hole will serve to attract the cat's attention. Also scatter feathers or deer hair around the set.

BIRDWING SET
FOR BOBCAT

BOBCAT SCENT
ON BIRDWING

TRAP SET ON
SLIGHTLY HIGHER
GROUND

To attract bobcat from greater distances or from upwind of the set, hang an attractive tidbit like a bird wing or rabbit skin from a nearby tree.

If you can locate a cat "toilet" this is the very best location for any cat set. In forested terrain such areas are often found right in the middle of old, partially grown over logging roads. Bobcat will cross these roads at high ridges and knolls and deposit their droppings right in the road. If cat are using the toilet regularly, you may find up to a dozen droppings ranging from old to very fresh and numerous scratch marks in the ground. Bobcat will scratch and toss dirt over their droppings like any house cat. A cubby set, dirt-hole set, or bird-wing set made nearby has an excellent chance. A good cat lure will enhance any set.

Bobcat and lynx tend to prime later than fox and coyote and a lot of cat trapping is done after snowfall, when fur is in best condition. The snare set, where legal, is very effective. In the heavily forested areas of Canada, snares probably account for more lynx than any other kind of trap. The lightness of snares makes them an ideal choice when long distances on snowshoes in forested terrain have to be covered. This and the fact that the sets stay in working condition for long periods make them a favorite for deep snow trapping of both bobcat and lynx.

The cats like their meat fresh but in the winter months commonly feed on deer and other animal carrion. Often the cat will hole-up in a nearby brush pile during the day and each night walk to the carrion to feed—walking in exactly the same tracks each night. This is an ideal situation for the snare set, which can be set as recommended for coyote.

Because bobcat and lynx weights range up to 50 pounds, a good-sized trap is needed to hold them. A favorite is the No. 14 Oneida Jump. This trap has an unusually wide jaw spread. At least a No. 3 trap should be used. The No. 4 double longspring is another good bet. In fairly open country where drags are not advisable and traps are staked solid, a strong trap is needed to hold a wildcat. If a drag is used, a No. 2 trap will hold cats a high percentage of the time, but why take chances?

The bobcat and lynx are case-skinned. Stretching boards should be 4' long, about 9" wide at the base, and 7" at the shoulder. Bobcat vary considerably in size and larger size boards may be needed. After a couple of days with the flesh side out, turn the pelt fur side out and complete the drying process.

BADGER

Trappers after fox and coyote often wind up with badger in addition; however, traps set expressly for badger will add to the trapper's income modestly and for the hobbyist, it is a rather novel and unusual animal to trap. The principal use for badger fur is the making of shaving and artist brushes; the fur is also trimmed and used to dress up other fur. Skinned open and stretched almost square, the badger's pelt makes an interesting wall decoration. Gaining permission to trap badger on private lands is usually not difficult—most ranchers consider it a pest. The large holes left when it digs out gophers and ground squirrels are a hazard to horses and cattle. Once you have gained permission to trap badger, it is usually an easy step to gain permission to trap the same area for more valuable furbearers.

Broad-shouldered, bowlegged, pigeon-toed, the badger is built close to the ground and endowed with long digging claws that enable it to dig out—and devour—all manner of small animals. The loose fitting fur is long, grizzled, and multicolored: grey to white, black and silver-tipped. Head markings are distinctive: a white stripe runs from the nose over the top of the head; the cheeks are white and in front of each ear is a black slash. The feet are black. Length is 2'–3'. Weight is from 12–25 pounds.

Badger are found all over the western United States from Mexico into southern Canada and also in the Great Lakes states as far east as Ohio. The dry, treeless areas of plains and prairies are where the badger feels most at home. It breeds in the fall but because of delayed implantation the actual gestation period of some six weeks does not begin until February. The young, from one to five (two is the average), are born in an underground tunnel dug by the mother. Dens, or holes dug by badger in pursuit of small game, have the slightly flattened look that coincides with the animal's oddly shaped body.

The badger is a member of the weasel family and shares the disposition of these feisty cousins. The powerful claws and heavy body make it a match for most fox, coyote, even packs of dogs. Few animals, except the young and the foolish, bother the badger, who is able to give off a strong and obnoxious odor.

STRETCH BADGER OPEN

Small rodents in the form of gophers, prairie dogs and ground squirrels are the badger's main source of food, but the diet also includes rabbits, lizards, snakes, birds, eggs, insects, honey—including bee larvae—and to some extent it will eat carrion. The badger is a powerful digger and when after a rodent will disappear below the surface of the earth in seconds. Few small game animals and rodents can escape below the ground when pursued by a badger unless they find shelter in between rocks where the great digger cannot reach them. Badger undoubtedly do the ranchers and farmers a service by ridding the countryside of rodents but the holes left in their wake are often an even greater hazard.

The many holes dug in pursuit of rodents are an easy giveaway to the presence of badger. Look for this sign in open grasslands and pastures. In the more wooded Great Lakes states, badger will turn up almost anywhere. Frequently their holes will be seen along the grassy banks bordering railroad tracks, even in parklike woodlots used for pasture. But favorite areas are the open, sometimes rather arid country populated by pocket gophers, ground squirrels, and similar burrowing rodents.

When a badger smells the odor of ground squirrels in a tunnel and burrows down to the rodents' nest and devours them, it may remain in its access tunnel, spending the day in the coolness before emerging to hunt again that night. As a result, a freshly dug badger tunnel is sometimes considered to be a good set location. However, the badger will often leave so many freshly dug holes in an area during a night's work that picking the right one can be difficult. Even if an occupied tunnel is selected, the badger, when emerging, often bulldozes a wave of dirt ahead of it as it leaves the hole and this almost always springs the trap.

The common dirt-hole set will take badger, but when making the set expressly for badger two traps should be used and set side by side to catch this rather oddly shaped animal. Its feet are so wide apart and it is so bowlegged that when walking straight into a dirt-hole set in its usual way, the animal may straddle a single trap with its legs and sometimes even set off the trap with its belly.

The Bank-Hole Set

Probably the most efficient way to trap badger is with the baited bank-hole set. Make this set in an area where there is plentiful badger sign. Look for an old hole along the side of a ditch bank or dry wash. If no natural hole is available, dig one about 2′ deep and 1½′ wide. Put a bait of rabbit, bird, or even an opened can of sardines in the back of the hole. Dig a trap bed large enough for two No. 2 or No. 3 traps. Set the traps and stake solidly. After inserting a trap covering of wax paper or canvas over the trap pans (extending under the trap jaws), sift a fine layer of dirt over the traps. Almost any kind of animal lure can be used with a

BANK HOLE SET FOR BADGER

badger set if it holds the promise of food or simply entices the badger's curiosity.

The badger is skinned open. The pelt is stretched as nearly square as possible on a flat board with the flesh side up.

MARTEN

Some of the most fascinating trapping stories are woven around men who spent their winters locked in high country while trapping the marten. The marten is related to the very valuable Russian sable and the pelt commands a high market value. Although they are easy animals to trap, keeping traps—and sometimes the trapper himself—in working condition is a test of woodsmanship and grit. Marten like heavily forested terrain and high country, usually 4,000 to 7,000 feet altitude in the winter. Trappers will work out of tiny log cabins and face the constant threat of howling blizzards and arctic cold. When you take on the marten, you are assured of trapline adventure.

The marten is a member of the weasel family and has the long, slender lines of the tribe; larger than the mink but smaller than the fisher, it may weigh up to 6 pounds. The fur is long and silky, a deep chocolate brown with an orange or white spot under the chin. Legs, the rather prominent ears, and bushy tail are quite dark. Each foot has five toes.

The marten is found throughout Canada and Alaska. In the United States, harvestable numbers are limited to the Rocky Mountains, Pacific Northwest, and the extreme Northeast. They seem to be returning to the Adirondacks and occasionally appear in the Great Lakes states.

Marten breed in the summer but implantation is delayed and the young are not born until the following year, after a period of 225 to 265 days. The young, three to four on the average, are born in March or April in a hollow tree or other sheltered nest.

The marten is incredibly fast and can move with wild abandon from tree branch to tree branch; it can even overtake and kill a red squirrel in a tree. Equally efficient on the ground, it easily catches snowshoe rabbits and mice, but red squirrel is a favorite dish. The diet also includes birds and their eggs, an occasional fish, wild fruit, honey, insects, pine cone seeds, and carrion. The marten is hyperactive, a characteristic of the weasel clan, and seem constantly on the move, probing under windfalls and then, in a flash, flitting through the treetops. Quarrelsome among their own kind, it is not uncommon for a large marten to kill and eat a smaller one. This disturbing habit is a factor in keeping their numbers down.

The marten, despite a keen nose and sharp eyes, is not the least bit trap-shy. It will climb upon and use an uncovered trap for a platform when reaching for bait. Simple, easy to make sets are best for marten, but they should be made so that snow cannot put them out of working order. This usually means the sets must be made well above the snow level and in the shelter of pine branches.

The Leaning Pole Set

This is an easy set to make for marten; it can also be comparatively weatherproof. Select a pine tree with thick protective boughs and lean a pole against the pine so that the top of the pole is about five feet above the snow. Use your axe to level the top of the pole so that a trap can be set. Staple or nail the trap chain to the side of the pine tree. Now nail bait to the pine tree above the trap: red squirrel, rabbit, a skinned-out muskrat, sardines, canned cat food or salmon, almost anything that smells. A strip of rabbit skin sprinkled with food lure of any kind will do the trick. Bait and trap should be set below thick pine boughs. You can add to the protection against snow by cutting pine boughs and laying them crossways on overhead branches above the bait and trap.

These added pine boughs not only serve to help keep the set snowproof but help conceal the bait from Canada jays and other nuisance birds. An actual cubby above the ground can be formed by propping pine boughs and bait on both sides of the trap as well as overhead. The set is now even more concealed from birds but if there are marten around one of these inquisitive animals will find the bait and scramble into the waiting trap.

As in weasel trapping, there are many simple sets that will take marten. The only problem is keeping them working despite snow, hungry birds, and rodents. If the trapper is familiar with the country he plans to trap and knows where marten tracks are likely to appear after snowfall,

LEANING POLE SET
FOR MARTEN

DEAD SQUIRREL
USED AS BAIT

he can prepare fairly substantial cubbies before the season opens. Sometimes it is tempting to place bait and trap in a natural rock crevice near ground level and sets like this will pay off as long as they are not buried in deep snow. The thing to remember when making sets near the ground or snow level is to mark the sets with a tag tied well above the ground so they can be dug out after a high country blizzard. Better yet, keep your marten sets high above the snow and in the shelter of pine boughs. Traps are usually anchored so that a trapped marten will hang above the ground. In subzero temperatures a marten will quickly freeze to death and the carcass will be safe from mice and shrews who might otherwise damage the fur.

Plenty of trappers believe that the No. 1 size trap or even the No. 0 is okay for marten if suspended above the ground. The No. 1½ underspring "jump" trap is an even better bet and a size the trapper will probably have on hand from trapping mink earlier in the fall. Trappers are experimenting with good results with the body-grip trap for marten in the size normally used for mink and muskrat. Sometimes the body-grip trap is set in front of a cubby entrance in the same way that one would place a leg-hold trap. Sometimes it is placed inside a cubby or simply propped on the snow with bait on the trigger. One good bait is a three-inch strip of rabbit skin wrapped around the trigger of a body-grip trap and scented with liquid mink bait. A marten caught in the body-grip trap is not likely to escape.

The marten is case-skinned. Most fur buyers prefer buying marten with the fur side out. This way they can examine the fur more closely; it can vary considerably in color and quality. The best procedure is first to put the pelt on a stretching board, flesh side out, and let it dry overnight and then, while the pelt is still soft and flexible, turn it and complete the drying process with the fur side out. Stretching boards for marten should be 30″ long, a little over 4″ wide at the base and 3½″ wide at the shoulder.

FISHER

Even more demanding of wild, heavily forested terrain than marten is the fisher, also a member of the weasel family and, in fact, nothing more than a large marten. No one seems to know why it is called fisher since fish plays less of a role in its diet than in that of the marten or other weasels. Faster in the treetops than any other North American mammal, the fisher can catch a marten and not infrequently dines on this close relative. It is no wonder that members of the weasel family tend to be solitary wanderers; given the advantage they do not hesitate to kill one another.

The fisher is extremely rare. Naturalists love to expound that the fisher's range probably went as far south as South Carolina before the bad guys (trappers) caused its demise in these areas. It would seem that encroaching civilization had nothing to do with it. Adaptability is the name of the game in wildlife survival and those animals demanding of wild terrain untouched by human hands are going to be rare creatures whether they are trapped or protected. Unless you live in one of the heavily forested areas of Canada or the United States there is little chance of your being able to trap this super weasel legally. Where found, it is not particularly difficult to trap.

The fisher is almost foxlike in appearance, indeed, it is sometimes called the black fox but most would agree that it is more similar to the marten. Length varies from 34″–40″—over 12″ of which is tail—and weigh from 8–12 pounds on the average. The male may be twice the size of the female and weigh up to 20 pounds. Coloration is generally a dark brown, sometimes almost black, with a hint of grey. The fur of the female is much silkier than that of the male and pelts of prime females bring the best prices.

The fisher is found in parts of every Canadian province and in the northern woodlands of the United States. You can cross their track in Minnesota, the New England states, the Adirondacks, the Rocky Mountains, and the Pacific Northwest. But nowhere is it common, not even in the wildest of woodlands.

When a female fisher's young, the average is three to four, are only a few days old she will go out and seek a mate for next year's litter. There is delayed implantation and it is many months after breeding before the real gestation begins. The young are born in April, usually in a hollow tree or other dry nest.

Just as the marten likes dense spruce forests in high country so does the fisher favor such high, densely forested country, but it will also be found in lowlands as long as there are dense forests for it to live and hunt in.

The fisher is the only animal that habitually dines on porcupines. It kills the porky by deftly flipping the animal onto its back and biting it in the throat, then tearing open the soft underbelly to feed. Occasionally a few quills are picked up but these generally work free in time. Small game comprise a fisher's diet and include rabbits, marmots, beavers, birds, and a variety of small rodents. Anything not eaten is buried for future use. The fisher will eat carrion or bury it for a later meal.

Like every member of the weasel clan the fisher is a terrific fighter. These solitary creatures can rarely get along with other animals, even members of their own kind. In all of the United States and Canada only 8,000–9,000 fisher are trapped each year. This is a low figure when you consider that almost 200,000 mink were trapped in Louisiana in one year in the 1970s.

The Cubby Set

The baited cubby set, constructed near the hunting circuit of a fisher, will take this sometimes rather far-ranging furbearer. As with all cubbies, the one for fisher should be constructed with materials found at the set location. This is often a combination of logs and pine boughs. Sometimes a natural cave can be found or a niche or natural enclosure of any kind can be utilized. Sometimes sticks and pine boughs can be leaned against a windfall. The cubby should be at least 2' high and the entrance 1' wide.

The trap is set in the entrance and lightly covered with dirt or finely rotted vegetation. The trap intercepts the fisher when it tries to investigate the bait placed in the rear of the cubby. The cubby serves to protect the trap and bait from the elements and from predatory birds. Bait may be rabbit, porcupine, skunk, skinned-out carcass of muskrat (a favorite bait for many species), venison scraps, other meat scraps, or just about anything that promises a meaty meal. Mink or fox urine or urine from almost any other furbearer will help to lure fishers to your sets. Fisher can also be taken in trail sets and log crossing stream sets. Each foot has five toes, the claws of which show distinctly in the tracks. In deep snow, fisher tracks look very much like giant mink tracks. Traps set for fisher should be No. 2 or No. 3 size. It is usually best to use a stout pole drag. Fisher are case-skinned and, like marten, the pelt is first dried overnight with the

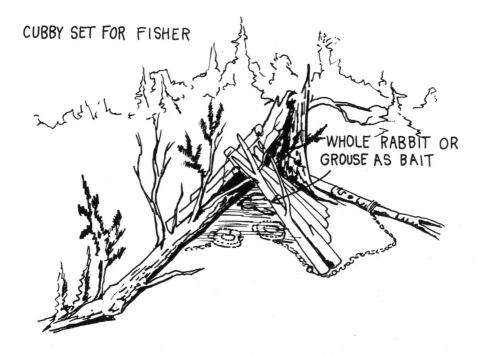

CUBBY SET FOR FISHER

WHOLE RABBIT OR GROUSE AS BAIT

flesh side out, then turned and dried with the fur side out. Fur color and quality will vary with fisher and fur buyers like to see what they are getting. The blacker the pelt, the more money it's worth. A light brown coloration decreases the value. Wood fur stretchers for fisher should be 40″ long, 7″ wide at the base and 6″ wide at the shoulder.

WOLVERINE

Few readers of this book will ever have the opportunity to trap the wolverine, which lives in the far reaches of Canada, Alaska, and the Arctic. It has the reputation of being an evil-smelling monster, able to elude traps with almost human ingenuity while robbing traplines of both bait and trapped animals; not uncommonly it breaks into trapper's cabins and food caches and what isn't broken or stolen is befouled with its musk. Surprisingly, the doings attributed to the wolverine are true. Its ability to elude traps, however, is probably more a case of the traps being small ones from which it can easily escape. It has been known to bury a trap and spray the spot with musk—this has given the impression that the wolverine is an evil spirit as well as a malevolent, oversized member of the weasel clan.

This fierce little beast is known to drive wolves, bears, and mountain lions from their kills, despite the fact that it rarely weighs over 40 pounds. Probably, the noxious odor, closely akin to that of the skunk, has a considerable influence in these matters as well as a ferocious attitude.

Wolverine   *(Courtesy, Pete Czura)*

Wolverine reportedly take caribou, mountain sheep, and goats—the sick, the young, and the old—it has even been said that this mighty mite has killed moose bogged down in deep snow. That is difficult to believe. Often shot or trapped to prevent the theft of valuable furbearers from the trapline, the pelt of the wolverine will bring a handsome price. The fur is generally used for trimming parka hoods because it does not freeze when moist.

The wolverine looks even less like a member of the weasel family than does the badger. In fact, it looks like a small bear that crossed with a skunk. Length averages about 3′ and it may stand as much as 14″ at the shoulder. Weight varies between 20 and 35 pounds but wolverine up to 50 pounds have been reported. Color is dark brown to black; the head is broad and the jaws powerful. Two yellow stripes start on each shoulder and meet on the rump. Although its back is arched, the wolverine's general appearance is shaggy and squat; it definitely lacks the sinuous lines of most members of the weasel family. However, it possesses the ferocity and ill-temper of the clan and, like other weasels, generally travels alone.

The wolverine is found from the Arctic Circle to the extreme northwestern corners of the United States; a few have been caught in California, Oregon, Washington, Utah, and Colorado.

Although facts are sketchy where the wolverine is concerned, it is generally thought they breed in late winter and the young—one to five in

NATURAL CUBBY SET FOR WOLVERINE

a litter—are born in a hollow log or other sheltered nest after a sixty-five day gestation period.

The wolverine hunts at all hours of the day or night and will take just about anything it can overpower. They are particularly fond of carrion. This liking for carrion makes a slightly "high" smelling bait a good one.

The Natural Cubby Set

A good set for wolverine is one where it appears another animal has stashed some food for future use. Find a natural crevice or hollow and lightly bury bait in the rear of this natural cubby. In some instances you may have to improve on the natural cubby with a few logs or rocks. Traps must be carefully concealed and covered with dirt, snow, or whatever is the natural material at the set location. Take the same precautions you would in trapping fox or coyote. You can stake the traps solid but it is usually best to wire them to a heavy log drag.

Trap sizes for wolverine should be No. 4 or No. 4½ in the double longspring model. The wolverine's evil spirit will not work on this powerful trap! Wolverine are usually skinned open and nailed flat to a board flesh side up.

Chapter
6
TRAPPING HINTS

Serious mink trappers prefer chest-high waders instead of hip boots. With waders on you can walk right down the middle of small creeks and streams. Thus you will avoid alerting the animals that you've been there because you'll leave behind less odor and you'll not disturb the bank as you might if you were wearing conventional hip boots. Chest-high waders are 100% better than leather hiking boots or having to make water sets by hanging over the edge of stream banks. During the warm weather you'll encounter in preseason scouting, waders are much less comfortable than hip boots. But once the trapping season comes, that extra warmth is welcome. Besides, they afford an even greater advantage by keeping you dry during a full day of scrambling in and out of creeks, streams, rivers, marshes, water-filled ditches, and lakes. No other foot gear or outfit will do that for you.

A lot of fox and coyote trappers wear calf-high rubber boots. They don't absorb and retain foreign odors as readily as leather hiking boots. Also, when leaving your car to make a set, you can clean the boots quickly by sloshing them around in a water-filled ditch or rain puddle. You can also add scent to rubber boots, scent that would not be alarming to furbearers, step in manure before walking into an unused pasture to make a dirt-hole set for a sly fox or coyote, or sprinkle fox urine on the soles of rubber boots. These odors can be easily removed should the occasion call for a trip to town.

Actually, the clothing worn on the trapline should, as much as possible, be reserved strictly for the trapline. If you plan a stop in town, keep shoes and clothing in your car for that purpose. Walking around an oil- and gas-stained garage floor while your car is being serviced is not going to improve your success on the trapline—such smells spell man and the world he lives in.

The kinds of gloves to wear for the trapping of elusive furbearers is a personal thing but trappers who stick to rubber gloves have pretty much the same good argument as those who wear rubber boots; they are easy to keep clean and you can easily add or remove urine or manure. Cotton gloves tend to be more comfortable in cold weather and by running your gloved hands over pine boughs as you pass them the odor of pine on the gloves is usually strong enough to cancel any foreign odors that might have been picked up. Generally it is wise to have two or three pairs with at least one pair always clean and hanging in a dry airy place.

Consider storing traps and equipment for an auto trapline in a covered box in the back of a pickup truck. If you drive a conventional car, the trunk may not be the best spot to keep your traps. Too often, car trunks are pungent with the odor of oil and gasoline. Car-top carriers are preferable; you can construct a wood frame across the carriers and bolt a wooden box to the frame. Use a swing open cover on the box for easy entry. Clean equipment, free of all odors, is half the battle when it comes to trapping the sly furbearers. Success is often just working out a system for clean, odor-free trapping. And odor-free means just that; even if the smell of rabbit or partridge is natural to where you live, keep any trace of them off your traps. These are food odors and will cause a fox or coyote to dig out the trap and, more often than not, set off the trap without getting caught. Steel and rust are, of course, the most damaging of odors but with proper trap preparation the only odor your traps will give off is a slight hint of log wood, an earthy, natural smell.

Some furbearers can be caught in unconcealed and untreated traps. Muskrat will crawl out of the water onto a floating raft set and step into unconcealed traps in attempting to reach bait of apple or carrot. Skunk and weasel will blithely walk into an unconcealed trap at the entrance to a baited cubby, but even these animals will walk around an exposed trap if it is convenient to do so. A light covering of shredded grass or leaves over the trap will do no harm. It could mean a trap-shy and valuable furbearer awaiting you in a set made for the more common and less trap-shy species. Do not overload a trap with grass or leaves, this could impair the action. Heavy leaf stems caught near the jaw's hinge can cause enough space in the center of the jaws for a toe-pinched animal to escape.

It is a good habit to carry a gardener's hand trowel and dig a trap bed for all traps set for land animals. This will help conceal a trap and also keep it level with the ground. The raccoon is not a trap-shy furbearer but when it has to lift its foot to get caught you're asking a bit much. Dig a trap bed so that the trap and the trap pan are level with or slightly below the level of the surrounding ground. If there is the threat of freezing temperatures with the result that traps might freeze to the ground, first lay a sheet of wax paper in the trap bed. Then set your trap and lightly sprinkle shredded grass, leaves, or rotted stump material over the trap pan and just a hint on the trap jaws. The trap does not have to be completely covered for the less trap-shy animals and sometimes not even for the trap-shy ones if there is no lingering foreign odor. A trap that is boiled and blackened in wood chips or dye blends in nicely. Traps set for the elusive fox, coyote, and wolf should be completely covered with a fine layer of dirt; in cold weather a layer of deer hair under and over the trap acts both to conceal the trap and keep it fairly weatherproof. A trap so covered will sometimes operate despite snowfalls and freezing and thawing temperatures. A few wise trappers scrape the hair off the hide of a deer shot in the fall and store it in gunnysacks to be used in winter trapping of fox and coyote.

One trapper who uses the floating raft set for muskrat almost exclusively, always cuts trap notches in the rafts to lessen the chance of traps being knocked off. He also puts a light layer of grass over each trap. He might do as well without the notches or trap covering but he is one of the most successful trappers using this set. It is difficult to argue with success.

Muskrats are active day and night. Traps set for muskrat can be inspected early and late in the day. This helps to prevent wring-offs—muskrats, more than any other furbearer, are able to twist free from the steel leg-hold trap unless stop-loss traps are used or drowning sets employed.

A stout stick with a fork on one end is good for dealing with small, live caught animals like mink and muskrat. Rap the animal sharply over the head with the straight, preferably smooth, end of the stick and then hold it under water with the forked end until all struggling ceases. This method of disposing of small animals will not damage the fur and death comes quickly to the trapped animal. Remember that almost any animal can inflict a painful and possibly dangerous bite. The little muskrat is particularly aggressive. Don't be careless with animals caught live.

Always reset the trap at a mink set after a mink has been caught, no matter how torn up the set may be. The struggling animal always scents up the set location and this is the best possible lure for attracting more mink to the same spot.

When following a small stream under a roadside culvert or bridge, mink will not travel the center of the stream but will always hug one wall. If the water is only two or three inches deep, set a trap underwater on each side of the stream and right up against the wall. If the water is too deep along one wall, set a flat rock in the water with a trap set on top of the rock and two or three inches below the surface. Such sets will take every passing mink, but they do invite thieves when set in these roadside locations. Try to inspect these traps as early in the day as possible to prevent your catch being stolen. Do not approach or linger at a mink set any more than is necessary. Once it has been established that no catch has been made and the trap is still in working order, quickly move on so as not to leave any unnecessary human odor at the set location.

Mink or muskrat will sometimes be found partially frozen in ice. Do not attempt to pull the carcass free as fur will be torn from the pelt. Cut through the ice some distance around the trapped animal and lift the animal and the surrounding layer of ice—the trap too if it is frozen to the mass—and carry to your car and allow the ice to thaw gradually from the carcass.

A trap wired to a narrow tree root or stake will hold most mink and muskrat but should a raccoon step into the trap you stand to lose not only the raccoon but the trap as well. Frequently the cause of the loss is the raccoon chewing through the root or stake; in fact, a trapped raccoon will chew through just about anything in sight but will not always put much pressure on the foot caught in the trap. Mink or muskrat sets made where raccoon are known to frequent should either be anchored to deep water or wired to a stout tree root or very substantial stake. Then, if the raccoon pulls free it will not take your trap too. A pole drag is normally recommended for raccoon but be certain it is hardwood of three to four inches diameter.

When extending the length of a trap chain with a single strand of wire, be sure that the wire used is strong enough to withstand the twisting action of a trapped animal. Clothesline wire is good. Light wire can be used to wire a trap chain directly to a stake or tree root, if several strands of wire are wrapped around the stake and through the chain loop. When the wire used acts as an extension of the chain and can be twisted, the strongest possible wire is recommended.

A good way to inspect traps set for fox and coyote is to use binoculars. Never approach sets any closer than necessary. If you left a lot of human odor while making a set for fox, this odor will dissipate in a few days *if* you keep a good distance from the set. If the trap has been staked solid, you can see from quite a distance whether an animal has been caught or the trap set off.

Carrion, such as a dead deer, is a very attractive lure for wolf, coyote, bobcat, and fox during the winter months when the snow lies deep and food is scarce, but ravens and birds of prey can spoil these sets by stepping into your traps. A temporary solution is to set your traps near dark. Birds will not bother the carrion after dark but hungry furbearers will. Unfortunately, the birds will return with daylight. A solution is to set your traps directly under the tracks of the furbearers you seek where they have approached the carrion. When the snow is deep, these animals will often approach the carrion each night walking in exactly the same tracks. Approach this single track trail from the side and scoop a hole in the snow that angles under the animal's track. Set a trap in this space right under the animal's track after first placing a sheet of wax paper in the trap bed and another sheet over the trap pan and under the trap jaws. The trap pan should just break through the bottom of the track in the snow. Sprinkle a little snow over this. Wire the trap to a log drag and bury this in the snow. Smooth out the snow as best you can. This set is fairly safe from ravens and other scavenger birds.

Tunneling a hole in the snow to set a trap right under an animal's track is a good method to take any of the larger furbearers in trail sets when the snow lies deep. It is one answer to deep snow fox and coyote trapping where snares are not allowed. A large trap works best with this kind of set. A No. 3 size trap will break through the snow more easily when stepped in by a fox than will the No. 2.

The next time you fillet a stringer of walleye, pike, bass, or whatever, drop the heads and other waste parts into plastic bags and store in your home freezer for the trapping season. When taken out and thawed, you have fresh fish bait that will attract a multitude of furbearers. Mink, while not inclined to take bait no matter how fresh, are still attracted by the odor of bait and curiosity for a closer look usually lands them in a well-placed trap. Fish is excellent bait for raccoon. In fact, few furbearers will ignore the aroma of fresh fish. As long as you package the fish scraps while they are still fresh there is no garbage smell that might otherwise taint your freezer.

Excellent bait for muskrat is the flesh of another muskrat. Some trappers have found it superior to apple, carrot, and other vegetable bait.

Two traps are better than one. This is especially true if you are making a set with old traps or traps that are too small for the animal sought.

ANIMAL TRACKS

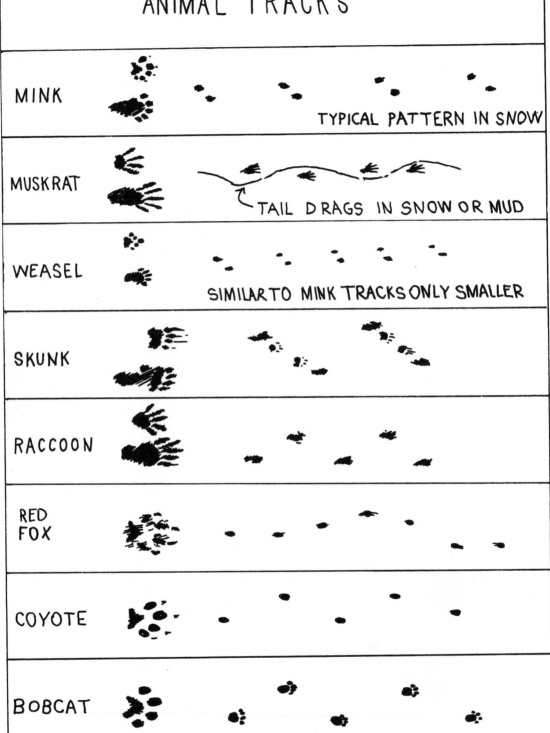

MINK   TYPICAL PATTERN IN SNOW

MUSKRAT   TAIL DRAGS IN SNOW OR MUD

WEASEL   SIMILAR TO MINK TRACKS ONLY SMALLER

SKUNK

RACCOON

RED FOX

COYOTE

BOBCAT

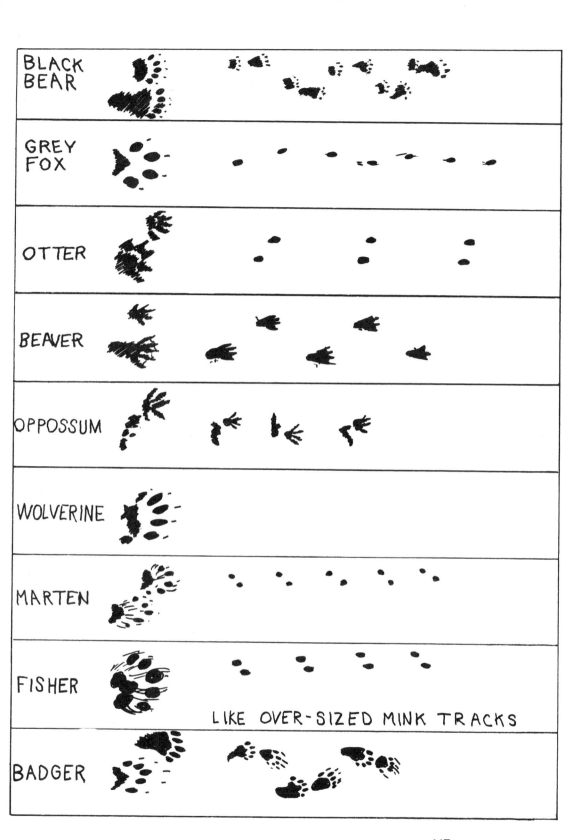

BLACK BEAR

GREY FOX

OTTER

BEAVER

OPPOSSUM

WOLVERINE

MARTEN

FISHER

LIKE OVER-SIZED MINK TRACKS

BADGER

117

Chapter
7
HANDLING FURS

Wᴇʟʟ-ʜᴀɴᴅʟᴇᴅ animal pelts are things of beauty—raw animal pelts, that is. Few trappers are stirred by the sight of a fox fur collar or even a lush mink coat worth thousands of dollars, but a few prime fox pelts or a collection of fall-caught mink pelts hanging on a shed wall do something for a trapper's psyche. They conjure feelings of well-being and the good life still available to the trapper and outdoorsman. Selling pelts to the fur buyer is done with reluctance.

Proper fur handling begins before the skinning, the pelt of the furbearer must be clean and dry. Never attempt to skin a partially frozen animal; in fact, the furbearer that is still a little warm is the easiest of all to skin. In most instances mink, muskrat, weasel, and other small furbearers require only a drying out before the skinning job. Do not hang in front of a wood stove or other excessive heat. A temperature of 55–60°F above zero is about right for drying or thawing freshly caught animals or for the drying of stretched pelts. A light toweling with a piece of burlap will hasten the drying process of a pelt and remove any mud as it dries. Fox and brush-wolf may at times be hopelessly snarled with burrs; go over these animals with a dog comb. Do not, however, attempt to get the really hopelessly snagged burrs out. All you *will* do is pull out a lot of fur. Most fur buyers are aware that these can easily be removed at the tannery and will not offer a lower price because of it. After your furbearers have been dried and lightly brushed, they are ready for skinning.

There are two recognized ways of skinning animals. These are case-skinning and open-skinning. Most animals are case-skinned including weasel, muskrat, mink, raccoon, skunk, otter, squirrel (red squirrels are

118

trapped for their fur in many Canadian provinces), fisher, marten, fox, lynx, bobcat, wolf, coyote, and wolverine. Only beaver, bear, and badger are skinned open. At one time it was common practice to skin raccoon open and stretch the pelt as nearly square as possible. Today most fur buyers prefer raccoon to be case-skinned. The only animal that is open-skinned and stretched square is the badger. Black bear are stretched square but in most areas today the black bear is classified as a game animal and the fur may not be sold. Beaver are open-skinned but stretched round or oval.

Skinning the Cased Pelt

If you can skin a muskrat, chances are you can handle any of the furbearers that are case-skinned. The only thing different with a fox or wolf is having to remove a tailbone, which is no problem. For example, let's take a mink. It has a furred tail for you to contend with, unlike the leathery tail of a muskrat that is left attached to the carcass. If you can handle the skinning job on a mink it is safe to assume you can take on any furbearer that is case-skinned whether it be a wolverine in the Arctic, a bobcat in northern Minnesota, a raccoon in Pennsylvania, or a muskrat in Louisiana.

The skinning job is a lot easier if the animal is hanging off the floor. Canadians have devised a way to do this, they employ a small steel trap. The end of the trap chain is nailed to an overhead beam or high on a post, then one of the animal's hind feet inserted between the trap jaws. The animal is held firmly aloft yet it is moveable during the skinning process. If you are going to use this method, first put the mink's right hind foot between the trap jaws, now grasp the left hind foot and make a continuous cut from the left hind foot pad to the right. This cut will run down

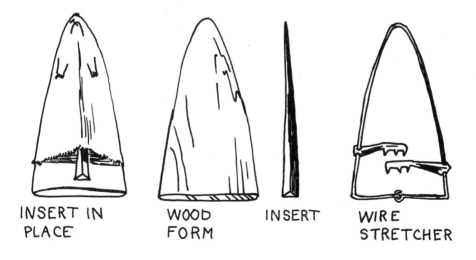

INSERT IN PLACE   WOOD FORM   INSERT   WIRE STRETCHER

and along the inside of the hind legs and pass just in front of the sexual organs and vent on the belly side.

Now grasp the mink's tail and make a cut from the underside of the tail, and about ½″ above the vent, down and past the right side of the vent to the first cut. Now remove the mink's right hind foot from the trap and insert the left hind leg between the jaws. Again holding the tail, make a similar cut on the left side of the vent. This leaves a V-shaped patch of skin and a little fur around the sexual organs and vent which are left attached to the carcass. On mink, and many other furbearers, there are strong smelling glands located at the base of the underside of the tail, just above the anus. If you do not start the V-shaped cut high enough you will pierce these glands with your knife blade and if you are, for instance, working in a basement or other enclosed area, breathing is going to become unpleasant. That is a mild description for one of the most nauseous odors imaginable. But if you are careful there is no problem.

The next step is to start working the pelt free of the hind legs and around the base of the tail. It is usually best to make a circular cut around the ankles of the hind feet to free the pelt from the feet. Once you have a couple of inches of the tailbone exposed, slip a wooden clothespin around the tailbone and, grasping the hind quarters of the animal with the other hand, pull the clothespin towards the tip of the tail. With any kind of pressure the tailbone easily pulls out.

The next step is to cut off the front feet and then start working the pelt down around the body of the mink. At this point, insert both hind feet between the trap jaws for a better grip. Work the pelt loose by pulling down with one hand while pushing in with your thumb between skin and carcass with the other hand. Sometimes the fibrous tissue between the skin and carcass has to be pared away with a knife but generally the pelt can be worked right down to the front legs without difficulty. When you reach the front legs, it is just a matter of peeling the skin over the elbow joint and pulling the leg free. Use great care when freeing the skin from around the head. A knife must be used to work the skin free. Cut the ears off close to the skull and take care not to cut the eyes and lips—suddenly the pelt is free.

Most fur buyers like the mink's tail split. On coon, skunk, and otter the tails are always split as these are very fatty animals and the tails might spoil if not split open and fastened flat to dry. It is a good idea to check with your local buyer to find out any preferences on how mink pelts and other furs should be handled. A favorite way to split tails is to take the grooved rib from an old umbrella. Insert this into the deboned tail and then run a sharp knife down the groove of the rib. This cut is done on the underside of the tail.

Fleshing the Cased Pelt

Fleshing of many of the smaller furbearers is very easy. Mink, muskrat, and weasel have very little excess fat. Slip the pelt over a wood stretching board flesh side up and with a spoon or dull knife, to avoid cutting the skin, scrape away the little fat around the head, shoulders, and hindquarters. Wipe away excess oil and fat with a piece of burlap.

Removing the fat from animals like the skunk and raccoon is more of a job as these are very fatty animals. The otter is even more work. The fat on otter is tough and gristly and no easy task to work loose. The job must be done however if the pelts are to dry properly.

Drying the Cased Pelt

Animals whose fur color is uniform throughout are dried on stretching boards flesh side out. The fur buyer can see by the fur that shows near the bottom edge of the pelt the color and quality of the fur. He knows this will be the same throughout.

On the other hand, animals whose fur color and quality can be inconsistent are dried fur side out. This is done by first putting the pelt on the stretching board flesh side out for a night or two or until the skin is partially dry but still soft and flexible, it is then turned and the drying process completed with the fur side out. The following lists animals dried with the fur in and those dried with the fur out:

Dry Fur In	*Dry Fur Out*
Weasel	Fisher
Mink	Marten
Muskrat	Fox
Otter	Lynx
Raccoon	Bobcat
Skunk	Wolf
Squirrel	Coyote
Oppossum	Wolverine

Pelts are placed on stretching boards of appropriate size and held in place with small tacks or pins. Small nails will be used for large pelts of fox or coyote. The boards should be placed in a fairly airy room with temperatures between 55–60°F. It is important to avoid contrasting temperatures of extreme heat or extreme cold. Do not remove the pelts from the stretching boards or wire frames until they are thoroughly dry. Then remove the pelts and allow to dry even further without being on a board or wire frame. If pelts are removed too soon from a drying frame they tend to crinkle and shrink. It may take a week for a pelt to dry properly. You may want to recomb fur on fox, coyote, and other animals dried fur side out. This gives the fur a clean and lustrous look. It may even impress a hard-nosed fur buyer.

Skinning the Open Pelt

The handling of beaver pelts is undoubtedly the most difficult task for trappers but, as with all things, practice makes perfect. A selection of well-handled beaver pelts is, indeed, a thing of beauty, and the size of blanket beaver, over sixty inches total from tail to eyes and across the widest part of the belly, is quite awesome to the neophyte.

To skin the beaver first cut off all four feet with a sharp knife or hatchet. On the tail of the beaver there is a flat joint near the first fringe of fur. Cut the tail off by severing this flat joint with a knife. Now turn the beaver on its back and make a cut from the underside of the chin on down the belly to just below the vent where the tail was. No cut is made out to the legs. The only cut is straight down the belly. The pelt is then skinned back one side at a time to the back. Be careful when working out the legs as the hide is easily cut in tender places. Cut the ears off close to the head. Skin around the ears and nose and the pelt is free.

Skinning a beaver is not particularly difficult if you do not worry about the amount of fat and flesh left adhering to the pelt. The removal of this fat and flesh can be a difficult job, however. Frequently there is no choice in backwoods country as beaver are heavy animals to carry and the only choice is a fast, on-the-spot skinning job. Expert beaver fleshers—like

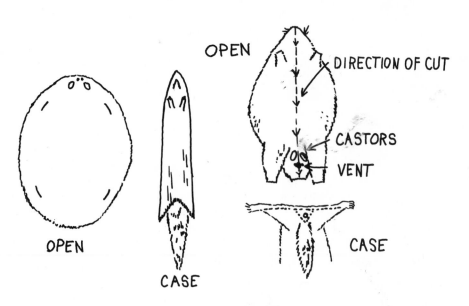

OPEN

OPEN

CASE

DIRECTION OF CUT

CASTORS

VENT

CASE

Rich Gilsvik nailing beaver pelt in the open-pelt style.

those employed by fur buyers, who have a good set up for fleshing beaver—can probably flesh one out in twenty minutes. If you have never done it before and have no special fleshing board or tools, it can take you all day to do one pelt, and it still may not be properly fleshed. One solution is to skin the pelt clean, leaving most of the fat, flesh, and gristle on the carcass. The belly of the beaver, where you first start the skinning job, has the least amount of fat. With practice, you can keep the whole pelt in this same condition as you skin it out. It takes longer, of course, but it can save time in the long run. It is not an easily mastered skill. Practice with a kit or some other low market value animal.

Fleshing the Open Pelt

A fleshing beam for beaver can be made from a smooth, round log of about 10″ diameter and 7′ long. Cut a notch from each end of the log so the ends can rest solidly on saw horses or stumps. One edge of the beaver pelt is tucked over the log end and held pinched in place. A curved, two-handled draw knife is the favorite fleshing tool of expert fleshers and skinners. You can also use butcher knives, broken glass, cabinet scrapers, and axe heads.

Drying the Open Pelt

A plywood board of 4′ x 4′ or 4′ x 8′ works well for holding anywhere from one to four stretched beaver pelts. Nail the pelt up by the nose so it hangs loosely and freely. Measure the overall length, subtract 12″ and draw a circle this size on the board. Use 16-penny nails to hold the pelt in place. Some trappers start at the nose and work around to the tail end. However, it is not a bad idea to start at the tail end—which is quite a bit tougher and can take a lot of strain without tearing—and work towards the nose. Use plenty of nails and follow the circle you have drawn. The nails should be placed about 1″ apart and the hide should be tight

WOODEN FUR STRETCHERS
(Suggested Sizes)

Animal	Length (in.)	Hip Width (in.)	Shoulder Width (in.)
Muskrat	24	7	6
Mink	36	4	3
Weasel	20	2	$1\frac{3}{4}$
Raccoon	40	10	10
Otter	50	9	$7\frac{1}{2}$
Skunk	30	8	7
Oppossum	30	8	7
Fox	50	9	$7\frac{1}{2}$
Coyote	60	12	10
Wolf	60	13	11
Bobcat	48	9	7
Lynx	48	11	9
Marten	30	4	$3\frac{1}{2}$
Fisher	40	7	6

between the nails, but don't try to stretch it because the hide will shrink as it dries. When these nails are in place, pull the tiny leg holes closed and nail into place. Beaver pelts should be stored in a cool, well-ventilated room.

Beaver pelt sizes are as follows: XX Large (Super Blanket)—over 65″; X Large (Blanket)—over 60″; Large—over 55″; Large Medium—over 52″; Medium—over 48″; Small—over 45″; Kit—under 45″.

All measurements are taken from the base of the tail to the eyes and then across the widest part of the belly. The two measurements are then added together.

Hints on Handling Furs

When tacking a pelt to be dried flesh side out on a wooden fur stretcher, first push the belly of the pelt slightly towards the head with your thumbs and then pull the back of the pelt down towards the tail before tacking in place. This will give the fur buyer a better view of the fur on the animal's back. This is not necessary on pelts dried fur side out.

On pelts such as mink, otter, skunk, and raccoon where you have split the tail, do not stretch it narrow and thin but work the tail wide with your fingers before tacking it down. This improves the appearance and thickens the fur instead of thinning it.

Before nailing an "open" beaver pelt to a board, be certain that the fur is completely dry. Wet fur held firmly against a board for a long period of time without the benefit of circulating air can deteriorate. The same holds true for case-skinned pelts on wooden fur stretchers.

When skinning a badger pelt "open" one must not only make a cut from the chin to tail as when skinning beaver but also make two crossing cuts: one out to the front feet, the other out to the hind feet, to follow the contours of the legs. This enables you to dry the badger in a somewhat square shape. Bears are skinned in the same manner but the feet are skinned out on bears and the claws left attached to the pelt.

Before fleshing cased or open pelts, hang the pelts flesh side out in a cool place until the fat has stiffened or hardened. This makes the fleshing job a lot easier.

When skinning beaver, save the castors. Found on both male and female, these are on each side and just forward of the vent. Remove these carefully with a knife or your fingers so as not to break the sacks, which would let the oil out. These should be tied at the cords and hung up to dry for they can be used for lure.

Dried beaver pelts should be stored flat. They can either be placed leather-to-leather or fur-to-fur, but should not be put leather-to-fur because this will make the fur oily.

The best hints for handling furs can come from a visit to your local fur buyer to see firsthand how he handles raw or unskinned furs. If he is not busy, he will probably be willing to spend quite some time with you—after all, it is to his advantage that you handle your furs properly and well. If he uses wooden fur stretchers, as most do with the exception of wire fur stretchers for muskrat, ask to borrow one of each size for the various furbearers. At home draw an outline of each on heavy paper or cardboard so that you can make boards of a similar size. If you cannot borrow sample boards, have a ruler handy and make on-the-spot measurements. Find out what furbearers will bring the best prices. Does he prefer the tails on mink to be split? How should the tail be held in place? Does he want the claws to be left on any pelts? Does he prefer raccoon case- or open-skinned?

If you have never skinned an animal before, there is no better place to watch this procedure than at a fur buyer's, because he employs only the very best skinners. By all means, whether you think you are a pretty good skinner or not, watch one of these men skin out and flesh a pelt.

A young trapper, willing to learn and not shy about asking questions, can quickly learn more than many an old timer. Strive to improve your speed and skill at skinning and handling furs. Be ready to listen to advice and try new methods. This goes for the whole trapping scene.

Part Two

PEST TRAPPING

Chapter
8
HOUSE and BUILDING PESTS

RATS AND MICE

The government estimates that in the United States alone there are fifty million rats on farms, thirty million in towns, and twenty million in cities. Diseases spread by rats have killed more people than all man's wars. Rats and mice gnawing through electrical insulation cause fires—and deaths—every year. Babies and small children are bitten by them, and rats cost Americans $200 million a year through the destruction of millions of bushels of human food. What rats and mice do not eat they contaminate with their pellets, urine, or hair. In one state a survey of cereal storage bins revealed that 41% of all stored grains were contaminated by rats, and 59% by mice. In one area of the United States only 3% of the corn reaching market was free from rat and mouse filth. In one state a chemist found rat hairs in 13 of 43 different brands of *canned* food. In another incident 1,800,000 pounds of sugar were ruined by rat urine. Are these rodents a serious problem? Absolutely!

The rats and mice that cause all this decimation and contamination are not native to North America. Our native rats and mice are saints compared to the Old World rats and mice referred to here: the Norway rat, the black rat, and the house mouse. All three of these villains are originally from Asia. They spread across Europe and then joined in discovering the New World. The Norway rat (not an original native of Norway) is the worst offender. The house mouse is rated second, the black rat third.

Rats and mice may live in colonies, particularly rats. They take a serious toll of wildlife, pets, and domestic stock. Ground nesting birds and

The Norway rat is king of pests.

small mammals are easy prey. A lone rat will kill hundreds of chicks in a single raid on a hen house. Gangs of rats will kill young pigs and lambs.

Rats and mice thrive where they have a plentiful food supply as in garbage dumps, tenements, stores, ships, and docks. They will live in hollow walls in homes and in adjacent sewer pipes. Brush piles or firewood stacked against the side of a house are natural hangouts. You may first learn of their presence by gnawing sounds and the scuttling of tiny feet in the walls. Worse, you may find where they have nibbled on a loaf of bread or eaten a hole in a wedge of cheese. Black pellets in the pantry or under the sofa signal rodents, usually the house mouse.

Not every rat carries plague or typhus-bearing parasites, infectious jaundice, or tapeworm infection which can be spread to man. Rats found around the farm or grain elevator are going to be cleaner animals than those inhabiting the tenements, dumps, and sewers of towns and cities. But in either case they are unwanted and unneeded by man or the balance of nature. Their total extermination would be to the good of all, but this is an unlikely dream. Although Indian legend has it that the coyote will be the last animal on earth, it seems more likely that rats and mice will have that distinction.

Rats and mice require little description. The Norway or brown rat is a pale, greyish-brown color, 13″–18″ long. A 16″ rat will normally have a body length of about 9″ and a sparsely furred tail of 7″. The house mouse will have a total length of 6″–8″.

Rats and mice are found wherever man has settled.

Traps for Rats and Mice

Trapping is a practical way to remove rats and mice. Poisons can be used but they involve potential dangers to animals and people, and odors can result from dead rodents. The best trap for rats and mice is the common snap trap, which kills instantly. Sizes for both rats and mice are generally available at hardware and other stores.

The steel leg-hold trap can also be used for trapping rats in sizes No. 0 to No. $1\frac{1}{2}$. Bait can be smeared or tied on the trap pan or the trap can be set in runways.

Trapping Methods

Rats and mice are accustomed to human odors and no special trap preparations are necessary. The smell of dead individuals does not warn other rats away. The slyness sometimes attributed to rats in avoiding traps is really a case of its being difficult to squelch their numbers. If you catch 95%, the remaining 5% will quickly restore their loss through prolific breeding.

Many foods make good bait for rats and mice. Peanut butter and cheese are two favorites, others include nutmeats, doughnuts, cake, fried bacon, raisins, strawberry jelly, and soft candies, particularly milk chocolate and gumdrops. You can also sprinkle rolled oats over and around the bait trigger. Oats and other grains may work better if you enlarge the bait pan with a piece of cardboard or light screen wire. Cut the cardboard or screen in a square shape slightly smaller than the edge of the guillotine wire and attach it firmly to the bait pan. This will work on both mouse and rat traps.

The Victor brand mouse trap is available with the wooden pedal impregnated with nontoxic scent designed to attract mice, thus eliminating the need for baiting by the purchaser.

"Trap-shy individuals may be caught," the U.S. Department of Interior notes, "by hiding the entire trap under a layer of flour, dirt, sawdust, fine shavings, or similar lightweight material."

Mice are the rodent most commonly trapped in the home. Nothing is easier to catch but people often make the same mistake: they see a mouse running, for example, across the center of the kitchen floor, and they proceed to set a baited trap right in the center of the floor. The only reason the mouse ran across the open expanse of floor in the first place was because he was frightened. Mice are timid. They will not approach bait set out in the center of a room. Set your traps flush with a wall, and preferably a section of wall behind a stove or refrigerator, or any furniture or appliance. The narrow space between a stove or refrigerator and the kitchen wall is a natural runway for these tiny rodents. Often there is also spilled food lying behind these obstructions, food that does not always get cleaned up. In such a sheltered nook, a baited trap will be approached without hesitation, so set several.

If the traps have been set in the evening and you plan to be up for a while, turn the lights off in the room where the mouse was seen and the traps are set. Chances are you will have the mouse, and maybe others, within thirty minutes. They are easy to catch with proper trap placement.

In the basement, barn, or shed, rats and mice still travel along walls, particularly walls located behind large objects that provide cover. Baited traps are set in these sheltered runways. Where animals travel on rafters or pipes, nail the traps in place or wire them to pipes, set several!

Rats and mice come readily to strategically placed baited traps, but in a situation where there is a lot of food available to them it helps to force the rat or mouse to run over your trap in its travels. You can pinpoint the travel routes of mice and rats by sprinkling talcum powder, flour, or similar material in foot-square patches in likely places. Use boxes or other obstacles to force the rat or mouse to pass over the trap trigger. Put two snap traps side by side to cover a runway for even better results. The enlarged bait pan works well in runway trapping. To protect pets and small children, prop cardboard boxes over the traps with space below for the rodents to enter, or place traps out of reach. The snap trap is particularly powerful in the rat size and could break small fingers. Handle rats and mice with gloves and bury the carcasses.

SKUNK

Skunk have the annoying habit of making their burrows under lakeside cottages, house porches, barns, sheds, and wood or brush piles. They are beneficial animals in many respects, ridding an area of many rodents and insects, but sooner or later you or a domestic animal is going to startle one of these slow-to-anger animals and then it will unleash its vile smelling defensive spray on the premises. This usually stirs the most fawning of animal lovers into considering the possibility of getting the darn things off his immediate property.

Skunk also inflict lawn damage. A skunk will dig at night in a well-manicured lawn for grubs and other food found a few inches below the surface. In one night a single skunk may dig twenty-five or more holes in the lawn, such holes are roughly 1½″ wide at the top and taper into the ground for 2–3″. On the farm they'll raid the henhouse for both chickens and eggs. They are also a threat to the eggs of gamebirds such as partridge, pheasant, and quail.

Skunk are easy to trap, the only problem is in dispatching the animal before it releases its defensive spray. (Skunk can be live-trapped and safely transported to outlying fields and woodlands. This is discussed in Part Three.) A trap worth trying on skunk is the Victor Conibear body-grip trap in the No. 220 size. If it catches the skunk just right it can result in the animal's demise without any musk being released. Set the trap in the entrance to the skunk's burrow. If there is no clearly defined and narrow entrance, use guide sticks or rocks to narrow the space so the skunk must pass through the trap.

The steel leg-hold trap is still a good one and the No. 1½ size is about right for skunk. Set the trap in the entrance to the skunk's burrow and lightly cover with grass clippings. Stake solidly. The trapped skunk must not be allowed to retreat into its burrow after being caught. This will make shooting the animal difficult. Dispatch the trapped skunk with a .22 rifle or even a shotgun. Aim for the center of the chest or try for the spine just above the chest area. A spine shot is said to prevent the skunk's releasing any musk through convulsive movements, after being shot, as will often happen with a head shot. But even if a little musk is released, the air will clear within a few days. Reset the trap or traps until you believe all the skunks have been caught.

It is always a good idea to wear gloves when handling skunks or other animals caught. Should you attempt to pick one up that is not quite dead there is the chance of being bitten. Gloves will offer some protection. "Skunks," says the United States Department of the Interior, "are a reservoir in the transmission of rabies. In many states they have replaced foxes as the most important species spreading this disease."

A point to remember when setting any kind of trap in your house, yard, or adjoining property is that pets, particularly cats and dogs, can easily be caught. One solution is to set your traps during the evening hours only. Keep pets confined at this time. This is the time period when wild animals are most active. Set your traps off when you check them in the morning so your pets can run during the day. Reset the traps again in early evening after first confining your pets. Chances are you will be rid of any annoying pests within a few evenings of intensive trapping.

For additional information on skunks, their description, range, habits, and how to trap them, see the material on skunk.

One final note, as offered by the Department of the Interior, "Skunk odors on pets, clothing, under buidings, etc., may be neutralized by liberal use of a deodorant such as neutroleum alpha. The use of vinegar or household chlorine bleach in weak solution is also suggested for removing the odor from clothing or pets."

Chapter
9
LAWN and GARDEN PESTS

POCKET GOPHER

The pocket gopher is an endless burrower rarely seen above ground. A single animal can construct a complex of tunnels covering an entire acre. The main tunnel may be over 500 feet long with many lateral tunnels and storage chambers. A problem on cultivated, forest, range, or orchard lands, it will also enter a lawn or garden. It is frequently a pest in new suburban housing developments, in areas of light or sandy soil where undeveloped tracts of land remain between the clusters of new houses. New property owners find that young trees and plants wither and die. The culprit is the unseen pocket gopher who burrows in from the adjoining undeveloped land. There is little it will not eat in the way of roots and tubers. The only solution, aside from poison or killing it with truck or tractor exhaust fumes pumped into the tunnels, is to trap it off your property and in surrounding fields, pastures, or vacant lots. With a determined effort, even large numbers of these pests can be brought under control or eliminated. To catch only one or two in a home lawn or garden is a simple matter. In some communities a small bounty is paid for pocket gopher and farm youths pick up extra money trapping these pests.

A pocket gopher will seriously damage farm crops such as alfalfa by feeding on the leaves, stems, and roots from above and below the ground. Fruit trees can be seriously damaged in orchards where alfalfa and weeds have become established between the trees and thus provide a habitat for the gopher.

Root-cutting by gopher in forest plantations is frequently not noticed until crowns turn brown from summer drought or seemingly healthy trees are tipped at odd angles by the wind. These young trees can be easily pulled from the ground to reveal root-cutting and barking around the root collar. Beneath snow, pocket gopher forage above ground and tunnel through the snow to gnaw the bark of young trees.

Pocket gopher can be found throughout most of central and western North America. From 6½″ to 14″, including the almost hairless tail of 2–3″, the front claws are enlarged for the purpose of digging. Color is predominantly brown. This is a plump rodent with cheek pouches and yellow teeth, rarely seen unless in a trap. All you generally note is the characteristic mound of earth left at the end of each of the lateral tunnels.

Traps for Pocket Gopher

Pocket gopher are easily taken in the steel leg-hold trap. The No. 1 size in the underspring "jump" model is the easiest to use as it can be set in the gopher's narrow tunnel. You can also use special killer-type traps designed for gopher; directions usually accompany the traps.

Trapping Methods with the Leg-Hold Trap

With a pointed stick, probe for the gopher's tunnel a few feet from an earth mound left by the animal. When you feel the stick suddenly plunge downward without resistance you have found a tunnel. With a hand trowel, dig down to the tunnel and then enlarge it slightly so your trap can be set and the jaws operate without interference. Set the trap in the widened tunnel but stake the trap chain above ground. Next place a piece of cardboard or wood over the hole you have excavated and cover with the dirt dug from the hole. The idea is to prevent light from entering the tunnel. The pocket gopher is not trap-shy but if it notices light streaming into the tunnel, its first inclination is to start maneuvering dirt in that direction—this would result in a trap plugged with earth.

When a gopher is trapped, rap the animal over the head with a stick. Small children should be kept away from gopher sets because a trapped gopher will often struggle to the surface and will eagerly bite anyone who might be unwise enough to attempt to pick it up.

MOLES

The mole does not feed on plant and bulb roots as might be assumed, rather the damage to plant roots is done when the roots are dislodged by the burrowing mole as it seeks earthworms and insects, which form the bulk of its diet. The roots and bulbs in mole tunnels are usually eaten by mice or other rodents that use the passageways. Soils that contain many earthworms, insects, larvae, and grubs are attractive to moles and the removal of such may be of benefit to the landowner, but in a well-manicured lawn the ridges and mounds of earth left by these high-strung burrowers are an eyesore on an otherwise beautiful lawn. In the garden the mole is doubly despised but actually it is an ally in controlling Japanese beetles and cutworms. Unfortunately, the mole works incessantly, particularly in the spring and fall, and it is not unusual for one to dig 100 yards of tunnel in a day. Moles are found in open lawns and woodlands where the soil is loose and contains plenty of humus; dry, rocky, or hard packed ground is avoided.

Moles in one form or another are found throughout the entire eastern United States and Canada, and several varieties are found along the West Coast. They are absent in the Rocky Mountains. Moles tend to be short and plump with pointed noses and oversize front claws, the soles of which are turned outward. Almost blind, the animal depends on good scent and sense of touch. In fact, it's often hard to distinguish the eyes on a mole's head. The star-nosed mole is the strangest family member—its pinkish colored nose is star-shaped and has twenty-two tentacles, probably a great aid to the sense of touch. Moles and shrews are similar in appearance. The most obvious difference is the large front feet of all varieties of moles; they are obviously designed for digging. Moles produce one litter of about four young each year.

Traps for Moles

A number of specialized traps are made solely for trapping moles, the most common of which is the plunger, or harpoon, trap. Another style catches the rodent in scissorlike jaws, yet another uses choker loops. All are designed to kill moles instantly and are available at hardware and other stores.

Trapping Methods

Early spring is the best time for trapping moles. By midsummer the animals are deep underground. In winter they work below the frost line. When the ground is still moist in spring or after the first fall rains, you will note the ridges in the ground left by burrowing moles. If there are many ridges, walk along the edge of the lawn and flatten a spot in each ridge with your foot as you come to it. Then see which ones the moles raise again. Mark these for trap setting, since all runways may not be in use.

Mole traps usually come with illustrated instructions. If you do not have instructions, follow these guidelines:

Harpoon trap: After finding an active runway, level down a small section of the runway lightly with your hand or foot to make a base for the trigger pan. Set the trap with the two pointed supports astride the runway and inserted into the ground deep enough to prevent recoil when the trap is sprung. The prongs should be poised about an inch above the original runway. Raise and release the prongs several times before adjusting the trigger so that earth will not prevent full trap action.

Choker trap: Press down a small section of the runway with your hand or foot to make a base for the trigger pan. Make slits in the ground with a trowel for the loops. Set choker loops in the slits so that the loops encircle the runway. Be sure the bottoms of the loops are at least an inch below the original passage.

Always inspect traps after a rain. If the soil has washed away, leaving a space beneath a trap trigger, insert a chip or flat stone in this space to insure quick trigger action.

Do not leave a trap set in a spot more than one day if it fails to make a catch. Reset in another runway.

RACCOON

It is August and your garden of sweet corn is almost ready for picking. You decide to give it a few more days so every cob will be at its sweetest, most succulent best. Conditions are perfect for a catastrophe, one that will probably happen that night but of which you will not be aware— until the following morning when you walk out to view your once beautiful corn. This morning it looks like someone has driven back and forth through the corn with a 4-wheel drive vehicle. The damage inflicted by a family of raccoon in one night is enough to break a gardener's heart.

Big, robust animals, they climb the stalks until the weight of their bodies snaps the plant. The cobs of corn are ripped open and the raccoon takes a few tentative bites. If the corn is ripe and tender, it proceeds to feed, if not it proceeds to test another. But even when a cob is perfect for eating, it is seldom eaten completely, after all there are so many more. Raccoon become irrational slobs in their eating and destruction. A whole garden of corn can be ruined in a single night.

Raccoon are notorious as well for raiding henhouses and killing chickens and devouring their eggs. They are fine animals with coats of sometimes valuable fur but around the farm or even within city suburbs they are a pain-in-the-neck.

One solution for protecting your garden is to set traps out around the perimeter of the garden within a few weeks of the crop's ripening. If there is the danger of catching pets or livestock, use live traps as described in the section of this book on live trapping. Raccoon may be classified as game animals, so check with local conservation department personnel before setting traps. If damage has already been done you will probably be able to get special permission to trap.

Traps for Raccoon

As already stated in the chapter on trapping raccoon for their fur, an ideal trap for them is the No. $1\frac{1}{2}$ double coilspring, but most traps from the No. 1 through the No. 3 size will handle raccoon. Should one pull free from the No. 1 size, it will at least have lost his appetite for chicken or corn that night and probably not return.

Trapping Methods

Any of the sets described in the section on trapping raccoon for their fur will, when made around the garden, intercept raiding raccoon, particularly with good placement and tempting bait. If raccoon must cross an open area in approaching your garden they will generally follow a grassy fenceline or other cover as they move from woods to garden. A baited cubby along this route will catch the raccoon before it gets into the garden. You can add eye appeal to these sets by scattering worm-infested or otherwise ruined corncobs around, also corn stalks. Add some sweet smelling bait like peanut butter, syrup, or honey. If you have cats for pets they will not be tempted by this bait. A good raccoon lure will help. Traps should be lightly concealed with leaves and grass and wired to heavy drags.

If raccoon have raided your henhouse, try to determine where they entered the henhouse and set traps here, but also make sets that will intercept the animals before they reach the henhouse. You might use a dead chicken for bait. Always keep in mind children, pets, and domestic stock when setting traps around your property. The best method of killing a trapped raccoon is to shoot it in the head with a .22 caliber rifle. You can release a raccoon alive from a leg-hold trap and possibly it will not return but they are very powerful animals and you risk getting a serious bite. If you want to release an animal the size of raccoon it is better to work with live traps such as those sold by Havahart or Woodstream.

CHIPMUNK

Chipmunk are hard to dislike but occasionally they become so numerous as to become pests. They will enter lakeside cottages and may get trapped in the walls. They dig up newly planted garden seeds and bulbs and attack cultivated fruits, seeds or stones—a strawberry patch is dearly loved. Trapping is the best method of control where a number of animals are creating a nuisance or damage.

The Eastern chipmunk and the Western chipmunk are similar but the Western variety is somewhat smaller. The Eastern chipmunk will average between 9 to 10½″ in length and weighs about 3 ounces. The Eastern species has three dark dorsal stripes, while the Western has five. Each is occasionally confused with the thirteen-lined ground squirrel, which is larger and has thirteen alternating light and dark stripes.

Traps for Chipmunk

The Number 0 steel leg-hold trap or the snap trap commonly used for rats is effective for chipmunk. The larger size leg-hold traps, No. 1 or

No. 1½, are not too large to catch chipmunk, and will close around the animal's head and body and kill it instantly. If you prefer to release the animals elsewhere unharmed they are easy to catch in live traps. See the section on live trapping for details.

Trapping Methods

Place traps around rock piles or logs most frequented by chipmunk, or near burrow entrances. Suggested bait materials include nutmeats, pumpkin or sunflower seeds, peanut butter, corn, or rolled oats. Nutmeats and other large baits should be securely tied to the trap trigger with thread. Rolled oats may be sprinkled around the trigger.

RABBIT

The cottontail rabbit does considerable damage to ornamental plants, gardens, orchards, and farm crops. It is also a popular game species. Before trapping or hunting this variety, consult your state game regulations. Snowshoe rabbit, found in the more northerly states and Canada, may abound in woodlands bordering on farms and even city lots but rarely bother a garden beyond nibbling clover on a lawn—that's about it. On the other hand, the cottontail is a nuisance even in winter, nibbling the tips off small bushes and ornamental plants.

Cottontail have several litters a year, four or five babies each. The cottontail has a greyish coat with white belly and white underside of tail. The less offensive snowshoe rabbit is more brown in color in the summer and white in winter. Chances are that any problems you have will be with the cottontail.

Traps for Cottontail

Snares made from picture-hanging wire and box traps are the best bet for cottontail.

Trapping Methods

Cottontail are simple animals but they are browsing animals and as such are not easy to lure into a trap with bait. The steel leg-hold trap is not recommended. A small snare loop formed with picture wire works best and usually kills the rabbit rather quickly. If you can locate where rabbits are slipping through a small opening in a fence or bushes, this is a good location for a snare set. The snare loop should be about 3″ in diameter and the bottom of the loop about 1″ above the ground or snow. See the section on live trapping for the use of box-type traps. Live trapping for release elsewhere is a good solution for controlling small numbers of these animals.

TREE SQUIRREL

Tree squirrel are another species hard to dislike. However, these small rodents can be pests. They will dig up garden bulbs, raid fruit and nut trees, damage standing corn as well as corn stored in cribs, kill or deform ornamental and forest trees by cutting buds and debarking, and their sharp teeth can cause considerable damage to buildings and lead cables. With the possible exception of red squirrel and flying squirrel, tree squirrel are usually protected game animals and state and local laws should be consulted before applying controls.

Traps for Tree Squirrel

The No. 0 or No. 1 size steel leg-hold trap can be used, also the body-grip trap in the smallest size such as the Victor Conibear No. 110. Permission, however, should be obtained from conservation department officials before using traps. Live traps are also used and highly recommended for ridding an area of small numbers of these rodents.

Trapping Methods

Set traps along frequently used pathways, tree bases, or rooftops where the animals usually run. Bait traps with peanut butter, nutmeats, sunflower seeds, or rolled oats. See Part Three for live trapping.

WOODCHUCK

The woodchuck is more often a pest in the farmer's field than in lawn and garden. But occasionally they raise havoc in gardens by raiding for carrots, cabbage, celery, and so forth. The woodchuck is a menace around livestock and cattle, the many dens they dig—and the entrances to those dens—are a hazard. In the spotted fever sections of the West, woodchuck are considered the distributor of the tick responsible for this disease. Newcomers to country life or suburbs do not always recognize a woodchuck when they see one.

The woodchuck is the largest of the squirrel family and weighs from 5–15 pounds. Length is up to 2', of which 4"–9" is a well-furred tail. Color varies but generally is a greyish-brown with a frosted look. The animal is stocky and appears a little clumsy.

Traps for Woodchuck

Set traps in entrances to dens or in trails the animals use to enter your garden. Traps should be lightly covered with grass clippings or sprinkled with dirt and wired to a heavy drag.

Chapter
10
LIVESTOCK and NEST PREDATION

When the carcass of an animal or the remains of a nest are found, the cause of the loss must be determined. Tracks and droppings nearby will provide clues but are not conclusive evidence. In the case of animal death, toxic plants and water, old age and disease, even destruction by farm machinery or by other livestock is a possibility. Predator tracks at the scene may only imply that they are feeding on the carcass. In one Minnesota community, conservation officers and sheriff's deputies searched for what turned out to be the phantom killer of a farmer's hogs. Later, when more hogs were killed the deaths were witnessed: the hogs were fighting amongst themselves.

The area around the carcass of a large animal such as a cow or horse should be examined for signs of a struggle. Usually tufts of wool or hair are extracted by the predator during the struggle. This scattering of material should not be confused with that spread by wind or by carrion-feeding birds or animals.

The loss of poultry eggs is difficult to pin down because there are so many animals that will take them including skunk, snake, magpies, dogs, raccoon, ground squirrel, and shrew.

Each predator species has a characteristic behavior pattern of attacking and feeding on prey. Predators of similar size and family grouping will often have similar habits. These will be listed together in the succeeding pages. Trapping methods that will take the one will usually do for the others in the same listing.

141

WOLVES, COYOTES, AND DOGS

These three will occasionally prey on sheep, calves, poultry, and swine. Livestock attacked by wolves will nearly always be hamstrung—seized by the hindquarters. If the livestock is carrying young, the animal will be disemboweled and the unborn young eaten first.

A sheep or lamb that has been attacked by a coyote will show signs of attack about the head and throat. The throat will often appear as if it was slit by a knife. Smaller lambs will be seized by the head and killed by crushing facial bones. Parts preferred by the coyote are the hindquarters, unborn young, and udder.

Dogs, like wolves, most often attack the hindquarters of animals. They rarely feed following the kill. Sometimes dogs and coyotes will cause livestock deaths by simply running around penned turkeys or sheep. The harassment by the predator from *outside* the pen causes the enclosed animals to stampede or pile up in one corner where some will die of suffocation. Look for fresh predator tracks outside the enclosure.

Traps for Wolves, Coyotes, and Dogs

Nothing smaller than the No. 3 trap should be used. Large and powerful animals like the timber wolf require a double longspring trap such as the Newhouse in the No. 4 or No. $4\frac{1}{2}$. Live traps are not effective for wolf or coyote but will sometimes catch wild or free-ranging dogs. Steel traps set for wolf or coyote must be deodorized by boiling in a bark or wood dye solution. However, rusty traps or traps with other foreign odors will sometimes do the trick because predators doing damage near farms or ranches expect a certain amount of foreign odor. Manure or other strong smelling substance that is not alarming to wolves and coyotes will help mask the odor of steel or man.

The best policy for the farmer or rancher is to thoroughly dye and treat a half dozen traps of suitable size *before* he has a predator problem. The traps can then be stored where they are not likely to pick up foreign odors and will be ready if and when needed. Trap covers, stakes or grapples, and a dirt sifter can also be kept on hand.

Too often predators are educated when poorly prepared equipment is used at set locations. If bait is used at these sets, the predator will not touch bait again, depending entirely on fresh kills. These are the smartest animals to trap. Do it right the first time.

Trapping Methods

Trail sets are good, particularly if you find where predators are crawling under a fence or slipping through a narrow passageway. Dig a trap bed and pound a stake out of sight below the trap bed or bury a grapple.

The trap should set slightly below ground level. Cover the trap pan and the area within the jaws with a trap cover. Sift fine dirt over the trap until it is covered to the original ground level, and blends with the surrounding ground. As you back away from the set, whisk out your tracks with a bush or pine bough. No bait or scent is used with a trail or "blind set."

For complete trapping instructions see the material on wolf and coyote in the fur trapping section of this book. Examine trap sets daily. Approach the trap site from the same direction each time, going no nearer than necessary to determine if it has been disturbed. If an animal is caught, reset the trap in the same place.

BOBCAT, LYNX, AND COUGAR

These three will all prey on sheep. Bobcat and lynx will take poultry, and cougar are known to kill cattle and horses.

Cougar will kill large animals by leaping onto their backs and biting the neck. Look for claw marks along the shoulder, side, or back of a dead cow or horse. They will disembowel their prey but normally feed first on the ribs or loin.

Bobcat kill sheep and lambs by biting their victims in the back of the neck. They prefer to eat the hindquarters of their prey first. The shoulder and neck region are also favored. Poultry are killed by biting the head, which is normally eaten. Both bobcat and lynx will prey on bird eggs.

All three cats have the habit of covering their prey with litter. Bobcat will reach out a little over a foot in scratching litter, while the cougar reaches three feet. The size of the bite will also help you in deciding if an animal has been killed by a cougar or the smaller bobcat or lynx.

Traps for Bobcat, Lynx, and Cougar

The No. 3 trap will do the job on bobcat and lynx. The No. 4 or 4½ Newhouse is about right for cougar. Check with local authorities before setting traps for cougar. They are now protected in many areas and special permission may be required.

Trapping Methods

All three of these cats can be trapped at the scene of a kill. Wire the traps to a heavy drag. The drag should be especially stout if the quarry is the cougar. The cats are not particularly trap-shy but it pays to make careful sets and to cover the traps completely with dirt or even hair or feathers from the kill. Because carrion-eating birds or mammals may stumble into the traps set at a carcass, make a couple of trail sets as well.

For more details on trapping bobcat and lynx, see the section on these animals.

BEARS

Grizzly and black bears quite commonly kill sheep and occasionally cattle and horses. Bear kill their prey by biting the back of the neck. The victim's underside is opened and the heart and liver eaten. The intestines are often strewn about haphazardly. Black bear usually attempt to skin back the hide of the animal to get at the firm fleshy parts. Bear droppings will normally be found nearby and flattened spots in the grass will be noted where the animal or animals have lain down to eat. The mere presence of bear can cause cattle to stampede.

Traps for Bear

Always check with local authorities before setting traps for bear, which are protected species in most areas. If damage has been done, permission to trap can usually be obtained or a professional trapper will be assigned to trap the offending animal. Traps used for bear are usually the No. 5 or No. 15 Newhouse Bear Trap. Never try to set one of these without the proper equipment, the consequences are pretty grim. A setting clamp, with a single screw mechanism, is provided with each trap, together with a small auxiliary clamp for holding one spring while the other is being worked upon. It is good thinking to leave these clamps in place until the trap is placed in position.

In Washington state, black bears do considerable damage to the inner bark of trees, and control measures have been used. During the early years of control, steel traps and hound hunting were used exclusively. Then Jack Aldrich developed the Aldrich Spring Activated Animal Snare which completely replaced the use of steel bear traps. The cable spring device revolutionized control operation because the snare was light, inexpensive, and completely harmless to humans. The device operates on the principal that when a bear steps on the snare's trigger, a $\frac{3}{16}''$ cable loop is thrown over the bear's paw and held secure.

Trapping Methods

Because of the danger to humans when using the steel bear trap, a stout cubby should be built with the bait and trap inside, and warning signs posted around the cubby. If the bear has made a kill, the remains of the kill can be used for bait. If this is difficult, many baits will attract the black bear including honey, syrup, fried bacon, fish, and just about any kind of raw meat scraps from a butcher shop. To lure bear from a great distance, burn old honey combs in a small fire built near the set location.

The sides of the cubby should be at least 3' high and built of substantial logs. Brush or sticks placed over the top will discourage carrion-eating birds. Lay a log on the ground across the open end of the cubby and set the trap just over the log on the inside of the cubby. Be certain to conceal

CUBBY SET FOR BEAR

the trap carefully and use guide sticks to ensure that the bear steps squarely into the trap. Bear are not difficult to trap but once one has its toes pinched and escapes, it becomes a very difficult animal to lure into a trap again. The trap should be anchored to a heavy drag at least 8'–9' long. If the small end of the drag is about 5" in diameter, the loop of the trap chain can be driven down around the drag. Once the chain loop is roughly centered on the drag, spikes can be driven into the drag to hold it secure.

THE POULTRY HOUSE RAIDERS

The following animals prey chiefly on domestic chickens, ducks, and eggs. When, that is, they elect to leave their natural habitat and prey on the farmyard. Here are some clues to their techniques.

FOX

Foxes can scramble over a fairly high fence to prey on chickens or ducks. Often the fox will carry the prey to its den, but it is not uncommon for them to kill more birds than they can eat or carry off. Eggs are opened just enough to be licked out and the shells are left by the nest. They often bite the heads off their prey.

WEASEL AND MINK

These two both kill their prey with a bite to the back of the skull, upper neck, or jugular vein. Heads and breast of poultry are eaten first. Both are noted for killing more than they can possibly eat. Weasels have been known to place many chickens in a pile. Eggs are sucked out through tiny teeth marks in the ends.

OPPOSSUM

Much mauling of the victim ensues when oppossum kill a chicken. Feeding is started at the anal opening. Egg shells are chewed into small pieces and left in the nest.

RACCOON

Raccoon have the habit of biting off the heads of their victims. They frequently carry eggs from a nest before consuming them.

SKUNK

Skunk are more interested in the eggs than the adult chickens. Eggs are opened at one end and the skunk then punches its nose into the opening to lick out the contents.

RATS

Norway rats kill chickens by biting their throats. Like other predators, they often kill more than they can eat and have a tendency to drag their victim to a corner or other sheltered spot before feeding. Rats have been known to attack and kill newborn lambs. The point of attack is the navel.

Traps for Small Predators

The No. 2 jump, coilspring, or longspring trap is adequate for most small predators. The No. $1\frac{1}{2}$ trap will also do for most small predators, with the possible exception of fox. Rats can be taken in the snap trap. The 110 size Victor Conibear trap is adequate for the smaller predators such as the mink, weasel, and rat. The body-grip trap is particularly effective when set in a small opening the animal must crawl through.

Trapping Methods

Methods of trapping these small predators are discussed elsewhere in this book, but frequently you can devise your own sets as dictated by the circumstances or conditions found at the site of their predation. Often there is a small space that the predators have used in entering a poultry house. This is a sure-fire location for a trap. On the other hand, it is always a good idea to intercept the predator before it gets that close to killing more poultry. The dirt-hole set, which is described in previous chapters, will take most small predators.

Part Three

LIVE TRAPPING

Chapter
11
THE LIVE TRAP

THE big advantage of a live trap is that it can be used to catch pests or even furbearers without injury to whatever is caught. Ridding your shed of a family of rats or removing a skunk from under your lakeside cottage leaves a sour taste if you also rid the family of a pet cat or even that friendly chipmunk the kids were feeding. Live traps are ideal around the farm, the weekend cottage, the suburban home, and even in city or town where unthinking neighbors allow their pets to run loose. Surprisingly, live traps come in sizes to handle even large dogs. Enough calls to a pet owner that the family dog or cat is in your live trap again can convince the most inconsiderate of persons to keep pets at home. It is also a handy way to hand over a free-ranging dog or cat to the local animal pound. Some people even use them for transporting pets or small numbers of poultry or other livestock. Live traps are used extensively for wildlife research. But the principal benefit is they can be left set in advantageous spots around the home, garden, or farm without danger to small children, pets, or livestock.

The two principal manufacturers of live traps are the Allcock Manufacturing Company, manufacturer of Havahart humane animal traps, and the Woodstream Corporation, manufacturer of the Victor/Woodstream Tender Trap.

Kinds of Live Traps

The Havahart line of live traps includes twenty traps, at least one carrying case, and several pet pens. Many of the traps are simply different sizes for different animals but special traps for live-trapping pigeons,

149

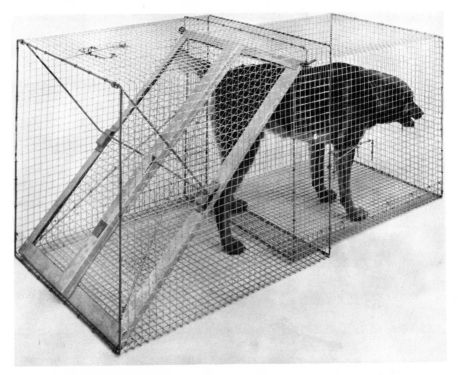

Live traps come in sizes large enough to handle free-ranging dogs.
(Courtesy, Havahart Traps, Inc.)

snapping turtles, sparrows, crabs, and minnows are also listed. Some are
real novelties, the Ketch-All Mouse Trap, for example. This ingenious
model can catch up to fifteen mice in one setting. No bait is used as the
small entrance hole is an attraction in itself, and once a mouse is inside it
attracts more. You can even buy a special drowning attachment that pops
the captured mice into a jar of water. Both the Allcock Manufacturing
Company and the Woodstream Corporation will provide, on request,
complete listings or catalogues. The Woodstream Corporation also manufactures steel leg-hold and body-grip traps and is the world's leading
manufacturer of traps.

Trap Preparation

Generally there is no special preparation required of live traps. However, when new and shiny they are not going to be as effective. Live traps
improve with age. Still, many small animals will have no fear of a new
and shiny trap. It is only when you seek more trap-shy animals that a
well-aged trap that has acquired a few animal and bird odors works best.
When using a new trap it is a good idea to wire the trap doors open at
first. When it is noted that animals are entering the trap and taking bait,

set the trap for action. Avoid leaving human odor on live traps as much as possible.

Indoor Use

Rats and mice are the principal indoor pests, but occasionally squirrels, chipmunks, and other small mammals will gain entry into a house, cottage, or outbuilding. In poultry houses there is the threat of rats, weasels, foxes, raccoons, cats, and dogs. If there are one or two small holes by which an animal could enter a poultry house, it is good preparation to have a live trap set up against each hole. All other possible entry holes should be blocked. In the case of a live trap where both ends can be opened, it is wise to leave only the end of the trap that is placed around

Washington state wildlife control personnel guide a black bear live trap into position *(Courtesy, Washington State Dept. of Game)*

A radio transmitter is attached to tranquilized bear by an employee of Washington State's Department of Game as an aid to studying the animal's habits.

the hole open. This will prevent any possibility of a marauder reaching the inside of a poultry house, granary, or whatever.

When a partly eaten chicken or other fowl is found, use the remains for bait on the trap pan so that a slight additional weight will spring the trap. If a catch is made, reset the trap—there may be others. Sometimes the culprit who killed the chicken will be a mink, which tend to be solitary, but sometimes trouble comes in many faces and the next day you may find a rat, skunk, or weasel in the trap.

152

RATS

In granaries or other places where there is feed for rats, it is well to keep a couple of live traps set on a permanent basis. An easy bait to replenish is a shallow cup of water balanced on the trap pan. Set traps along walls, under stairs, and in secluded passageways. Never place traps in the middle of a room. When possible, traps should be along the regular travel routes used by the rats.

A unique mouse trap that catches up to 15 mice in one setting.

(Courtesy, Havahart Traps, Inc.)

Rats are alert enough to be wary of a shiny new live trap. Bait the trap and then leave it set with the doors propped open at first so that once the rats get over their initial fear of this new object they will experience no problems when first starting to feed. Once you have caught a rat, the odor left by that rat will attract others and make the trap that much more effective. Check the trap frequently if there are many rats because they are often active day or night. You will be kept busy for a while disposing of the trapped rats.

Some of the better baits for rats include white cornmeal, rolled oats, scratch grain, peanuts, or cracked corn. Scatter these around the open ends and in the trap. A sure-fire bait to put directly on the trap pan is peanut butter mixed with molasses and spread on whole wheat bread. An elaborate treat for a germy rat? Perhaps, but it is one of the most attractive baits yet devised. Other goodies include cantaloupe, bacon, smoked fish, and even soap.

A good way to dispose of trapped rats is to drown them by submerging the live trap in water. Another method is to gas them with the exhaust from your car. Cover the trap with a piece of plastic and run a short piece of hose from the exhaust to the trap. This should be done outdoors. It would be extremely dangerous to yourself to do this in a garage or other enclosed building.

Outdoor Use

Outdoors abounds in places to set live traps. For example, around poultry houses, vegetable gardens, brushy fencerows, or the edges of woods. The larger size traps are especially effective for controlling free-ranging cats and dogs. Live traps can also be used to trap furbearers in nearby ponds or creeks.

SKUNK

If skunk are making their home under a building foundation or wood or rock pile, set a live trap nearby. If skunk are entering the yard at night, set traps along grassy fencelines or the edge of high grass or other sheltered routes that skunk and other wild animals are inclined to follow. Bait the trap with canned cat food (the kind that has a fish base), chicken entrails, cracknels, fish—canned or fresh—insect larvae such as May beetles, and fried bacon.

The best way to dispose of a trapped skunk is to drown it or gas it with automobile exhaust. A trapped skunk can also be carried some distance away and released. Surprisingly, a skunk caught in a live trap can be approached without the animal releasing its defensive spray if your approach is quiet. It is a good idea to drape a burlap bag over the trap if you plan to lift the trap to move it to another location for disposing of the skunk or releasing it. Do not shoot an animal while it is in the trap. If you plan to shoot a trapped skunk, first carry the trap and skunk a good distance from your's or anyone else's home, then set it free of the trap before shooting it. That way if it releases its defensive spray as it relaxes in death, you will not get complaints.

RACCOON

The raccoon is one of the slyer animals to lure into a live trap. If the live trap is the sort with a door on each end, set the trap with only one door open. The bait is then placed near the closed door. A small block can be placed under the bait pan on the side towards the open door so that it will not tip until the animal is beyond the center of the treadle. An adult

A skunk investigates
and finally gets caught
in live trap. *(Courtesy,
Havahart Traps, Inc.)*

raccoon is a large animal and you want it fully in the trap before it shuts. Smoked fish is good bait and will lure opossum as well as raccoon.

Special problems are involved with catching raccoon. The raccoon has long legs and very agile, almost fingerlike front paws, which it is inclined to use to reach through the side of a trap to steal the bait. This intelligent animal will even deliberately reach through the side to trip the trap pan releasing the trap door. After the trap is sprung, the animal tips it over, the doors fall open, and the raccoon enters and takes the bait without getting caught. To prevent the raccoon from stealing the bait from the outside or tipping the trap over—a situation that sometimes happens even when the animal is caught because its struggles can cause a trap to overturn—first pile rocks or cord wood around the baited end of the trap to prevent its reaching the bait. To prevent the trap overturning, drive a strong stake along each side of the trap or wire a long stick through the top to make upsetting the trap difficult.

Check traps set for raccoon frequently, as a trapped raccoon will damage a trap after being caught by biting and bending everything it can reach.

Good bait for raccoon includes smoked fish, canned cat food with a fish base, sardines, sweet corn, sugar-covered vegetables, cooked fatty meat or fried bacon. While fish baits work well for raccoon they are a problem where there are many cats around because after a cat has been caught, it wises up to this and begins trying to reach the bait from the outside. One solution is to use a bait of peanut butter spread on whole wheat bread with a little molasses or honey poured over it. A cat will not bother this bait, and although you may catch a few bluejays during the daytime, this bait will lure mostly skunks, coons, and woodchucks at night.

If setting live traps on bare or sandy earth, push the trap back and forth until the wire mesh on the trap bottom is covered lightly with earth. Some animals seem to be bothered by the feel of the wire under their feet, and this encourages them to try and get at the bait from the side of the trap.

(Courtesy, Havahart Traps, Inc.)

CHIPMUNK

The only problem with live-trapping chipmunk is that, more often than not, they become family pets. These animals tame rather easily, particularly the younger ones, but children should be cautioned not to try and lift a live one from the trap, it will bite if excited.

Set a live trap where the animals are most frequently seen. Bait the trap pan with a small piece of whole wheat bread spread half and half with peanut butter and molasses or a sweet syrup. Other good baits are peanuts and other nuts cracked and left in their shells. A good way to present the bait is to make a trail of small pieces leading to and through the trap. You may wish to prop the trap doors open at first to get the animals used to the trap.

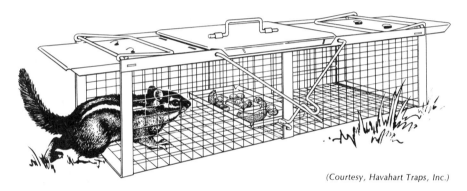

(Courtesy, Havahart Traps, Inc.)

RABBIT

Because there are so many growing things for rabbit to eat it is sometimes difficult to lure them with bait. The easiest time to lure with bait is in the winter when the natural food supply is low. Use fresh vegetables like apples, carrots, and cabbage. If you have killed a rabbit, a good lure is to be had by saving and utilizing the rabbit's bladder. By sprinkling a little rabbit urine in a live trap along with apple bait, you have a combination that will take most any cottontail.

Cottontail can be live-trapped any time of the year if traps are set right in or near trails in high grass or weeds. Note the route a rabbit uses when entering your garden and next time have your trap set to intercept it.

TREE SQUIRREL

As in trapping many other small creatures with live traps, it's best first to set traps with the doors propped open, so that the animals become used to them. Squirrels are not particularly trap-shy but if one squirrel is caught before the others have had a chance to get used to the trap, they will become leery of the trap from then on. So set your trap or traps out

(Courtesy, Havahart Traps, Inc.)

158

for several days with bait and have the doors propped open before finally setting for action.

If using the Havahart trap in the No. 2 size, which is the correct size for squirrels but a little small for some of the larger Eastern grey squirrels and definitely small for fox squirrels, one of the double doors should be kept shut. In this way the squirrel can enter farther into the trap before the single door closes behind him. A small block can also be placed under the bait pan towards the open door, so that it will not trip until the animal is beyond the center of the treadle.

To set these traps with only one door open, slip the straight door rod out from under the wire loop on the other rod. The door attached to the straight trigger rod can then be left closed and locked shut. Squirrels are not afraid to enter a trap set this way because of their habit of entering holes in trees and walls.

Bait with peanuts, sunflower seeds, or other nuts or acorns.

WOODCHUCK

It is usually in the garden that the live-trapping of woodchuck takes place. Chucks are most active in the early spring and this is also the best time to catch them. An excellent bait that will aid you in cleaning out every woodchuck and also every rabbit within your garden area is to plant a tiny patch of beans or oats. Set a live trap over the planted site. Prop the trap a little above ground level with rocks. In a few days the bean or oat sprouts will grow up through the open mesh of the trap. Woodchuck and rabbit are both crazy about these fresh sprouts and will enter the trap without hesitation. If there are a number of animals to be trapped, make several plantings of oats or beans, each a couple of days apart. The trap can then be moved as each new crop begins to sprout.

MUSKRAT

An excessive number of muskrat will quickly do damage to a farm pond by undermining the banks with holes, this will also weaken an earth dam. Live traps can be used to control their numbers and should be set around logs, stumps, feedbeds, and wherever the animals crawl out of the water. Bait with apples, carrots, or celery. Muskrat are most easily taken with bait in early spring or late fall, when natural foods are not abundant. If you plan to release muskrat live, take them at least two miles distant to ensure the animals stay in a new locality.

MINK AND WEASEL

Luring a weasel into a live trap is no problem provided that fresh, bloody meat is used. The flesh or organs of a freshly killed rabbit make excellent bait. Mink are a tougher proposition. One must seek out the places mink frequent along streams or ponds. A good location for a live trap is back under a pile of flood debris or any brush pile along a stream. Mink will always investigate such spots. Trap without bait should be placed out at least a month prior to the actual trapping season and the doors propped open so the traps can weather and the mink get used to them. As the time for trapping draws near, you can start placing bait tidbits in the traps and also start sprinkling mink urine or scent in the trap. Fresh fish and muskrat flesh are good baits. A special Havahart mink trap is made which can be set in water; instead of a bait pan it has a pointed wire on which a whole fish can be speared for bait.

Bait

The following bait are recommended by the Allcock Company, makers of Havahart Humane Animal Traps:

Armadillo: Meal worms, other worms, or insects enclosed in a little cloth bag; maggots, sardines, fish.

Cat or Bobcat: Fish, meats, oil of catnip, sardines.

Chipmunk: Prune pits, unroasted peanuts, corn, sunflower seeds, peanut butter, cereal, grains, popcorn.

Flying Squirrel: Apples, seeds, red rubber ball (an exterminator eliminated all the flying squirrels from a house using a Havahart trap and a red rubber ball for bait), whole roasted peanuts.

Fox, red and grey: Scented bait from a reliable fox trapper, chicken, rabbit (in form or live bait). Provide live bait with comfortable quarters, food, and water and place trap so that the fox will pass through trap in trying to reach live bait.

Gopher: Peanut butter mixed with molasses and spread on whole wheat bread.

Mice: Cheese, bread and butter, small nuts, cherry pits, oatmeal, sunflower or similar seeds, peanut butter mixed with oatmeal is very good bait, also gum drops, absorbent cotton, or flour. These baits are also good for rats.

Mink: Chicken heads and entrails, fresh fish, fish-oil scent, part of rabbit, muskrat, red squirrel, mice, fresh liver.

Minnows: Stale bread, popcorn.

Muskrat: Fresh vegetables, parsnips, carrots, sweet apples, oil of anise, or musk from another muskrat.

Nutria: Muskmelon or cantaloupe rind, ripe bananas.

Oppossum: Vegetables, sweet apples, chicken entrails, sardines, crisp bacon, canned cat food.

Otter: Fish.

Porcupine: Apples, salt, carrots.

Rabbit: Fresh vegetables such as brussels sprouts, cabbage, carrots, lettuce, or apples. In the wintertime, bread is a good bait. Vegetables

A commercial pigeon trap. Up to 10 pigeons can be taken at one time.
(Courtesy, Havahart Traps, Inc.)

have a lot of water in them and freeze in cold weather. Spraying the inside of the trap with apple cider has also proven effective.

Raccoon: Fish—fresh or canned—honey- or sugar-covered vegetables, smoked fish, watermelon, sweet corn, cooked fatty meat, crisp bacon.

Rat: Cheese, chicken or other fowl flesh, cereal grains, cracknels (made from bacon scraps or other fatty meats, these attract mink, weasel, skunks, rats, and the like), peanut butter mixed with oatmeal, peppermint candy.

Skunk: Chicken entrails, cracknels, fish—canned or fresh—insect larvae such as May beetles, crisp bacon.

A commercial sparrow trap that will take up to 20 sparrows at one time.
(Courtesy, Havahart Traps, Inc.)

Snake: Whole eggs (bantam), live mice.

Snapping Turtle: Fresh fish or chicken entrails, chopped. Put bait inside tin can in which numerous holes have been punched. Also pieces of fresh fish tied to trip wire.

Squirrel: Cereals, grains, nuts (especially peanuts, preferably not roasted), sunflower seeds, anise oil (a drop or two on bread). Peanut butter mixed with oatmeal or molasses is very good bait, popcorn, Milo.

Weasel: Fish, fresh liver, chicken entrails.

Woodchuck: Fresh string beans, sweet corn, lettuce, peas.

Voles: Peanut butter mixed with molasses, spread on whole wheat bread.

Birds: Undesirable birds such as starlings, pigeons, etc., may be taken in Havahart No. 1 and No. 2 traps, one at a time, using such baits as sunflower seeds or scratch grain run in one door and out the other. The birds follow the bait through the trap, which is tripped when they hop on the bait pan. Starlings are especially fond of raisins.

Chapter
12
HOMEMADE LIVE TRAPS

THE problem with most homemade live traps or box traps is that they are too complicated to work properly except under ideal conditions. Those discussed in this chapter are fairly trouble-free and the box trap in particular seems to go on working after other more complicated models have quit.

The Box Trap

This trap is made entirely from wire and will operate both in and out of water. It is a neat way to live-trap muskrats but is equally good for just about anything that will fit within its dimensions. For small animals such as mink and muskrat, the trap can be made about 30″ long x 6″ square. It can be made from 1″ square or 1″ x 2″ galvanized welded wire. The trap is made by crimping the wire over a board to get the desired square shape, then wired together. For large animals such as raccoon, fox, and badger, the trap should have either a wood or metal frame.

As with most live traps, the doorway is the key factor in its operation. Make the wire door 1″ narrower and 3″ longer than the entrance. This is a simple gravity operated door. It is not unnatural for a hungry animal to push its way under a slight obstruction to reach food it can see and smell. Hang the bait in the center and when the animal pushes its way through the swinging door to get at it the door drops back into position behind him. To release an unwanted animal, simply turn the trap over so that the doors flop open.

The Tin Can Trap

This is an effective way to live-trap rats and mice. Note in the accompanying photos that a mouse trap is wired to the tin can. Two holes are punched in the can and a soft wire run through these holes and around the mouse trap holding it firmly in place. The door is $\frac{1}{4}''$ galvanized wire cut to fit completely over the open end of the can. This is soldered to the guillotine spring on the mouse trap. The trap trigger that would normally fit into the trap pan is instead fitted under a stiff piece of wire—on the end of which bait is placed. This stiff bait wire is held in place by two cotter keys pushed down through holes in the can and then bent out on the outside of the can to prevent their pulling out. A close examination of the photos will help make this clear. A favorite bait is peanut butter or cheese on the end of the bait wire.

Pigeon Traps

Pigeons use regular feeding and roosting areas and can be controlled by intensive trapping. Set traps where pigeons commonly roost and where traps are not apt to be molested.

Small traps that catch pigeons singly are usually adequate for home and farm use but large walk-in types are better for controlling large numbers of these birds. Good baits are whole corn and grain sorghum. This should

The homemade tin can live trap in open and closed positions.

be scattered outside the trap door as well as liberally within the trap. Water should also be available in traps. If you are using large traps, one or two decoy birds should be left in the trap to draw other birds. Note that any trapped birds wearing leg bands should be turned over to their owners or the local humane society.

Loft Traps

The U.S. Department of the Interior points out that "Pigeons often use attics, unused upper stories in industrial buildings, deserted factories or partially used buildings as nest and roosting sites. These indoor roosts can be made into productive traps by closing them up with screening or plastic. Leave one or two entrances open until the birds become accustomed to using them. Then fit the entrances with trap doors which can be closed from the outside at night after the birds have settled down. The trapped birds can then be caught by hand or with nets."

Funnel Traps for Pigeon

An easy trap to make for pigeons is one with a funnel entrance using 1″ x 2″ mesh welded wire with a 1½″ V opening. Large nails are used to prevent this springing shut. Pigeons are lured by bait scattered near the entrance. They see more bait inside the trap and force their way through the small V opening. This can be made more effective if the funnel is at the top of an inclined board. As the pigeons pick up bait and finally squeeze through the opening they hop down five to six inches to the floor of the trap. This helps to keep trapped birds away from the entrance.

Bob-Type Trap for Pigeon

Very large capacity traps can be built that will catch and retain numbers of these birds. These can be made big enough to enable a person to enter through a small door constructed in the end of the trap and remove birds. But almost any size trap can be used.

The door or entrance through which the birds are lured is the main feature of this trap. Individual, free-swinging "bobs" are used. These bobs can be made of lightweight metal rods or heavy aluminum wire. It is important that they swing upward and inward easily and drop back smoothly into slots at the base of the door.

A Trap for Starlings and Sparrows

Starlings can be a real hazard in orchards, inflicting serious fruit damage. The U.S. Bureau of Sport Fisheries and Wildlife has done considerable research in controlling starlings in orchards and devised a center-drop trap that is easy to build and quite effective. It can also be used for sparrows which sometimes gather in very large numbers.

ENTRANCE TO BOB-TYPE TRAP FOR PIGEONS (METAL BARS SWING INWARD AND UPWARD)

The construction of the trap using 1″ chicken wire, is relatively simple. Side and end panels are covered with wire on the outside, top panels are covered on the inside of the frame. As with other live traps, the entrance is all-important. The Bureau of Sport Fisheries and Wildlife has this to say regarding the entrance, "The entrance (narrow slits in the plywood center panel through which starlings enter the trap) was perfected after two years of careful study. It allows birds to enter but is escape-proof. Therefore, measurements pertaining to the 1¾″ openings and the minimum 9″ allowance at both ends are critical and should be strictly adhered to."

CENTER-DROP TRAP

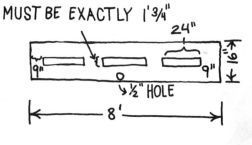

MUST BE EXACTLY 1'¾"
24"
9"
9"
½" HOLE
8'

Placement of this trap is all-important. Success in trapping lies in *correct placement* and *daily service*. Traps should be located in local flyways. Close observation must be made of movements and flight patterns into fruit orchards. Traps should not be set among trees. Select an open area where starlings in flight can easily see the baited trap and decoys. Ten or twelve live starlings should be kept in the trap at all times as decoys. Fresh water should be provided to keep them alive. An old tire split down the middle will make two water containers.

The Bureau points out that in some states, traps were baited with one or two boxes of cull apples. If apples are not attractive to starlings in your area it is recommended that other foods such as fine-cracked corn or a pelleted, complete ration food in a $\frac{3}{32}''$ or $\frac{5}{32}''$ size be used.

Trapping Information and Equipment Sources

MANUFACTURERS

Allcock Manufacturing Co., Havahart Box 551, Ossining, New York 10562

Blake & Lamb, Inc., Cambridge, New York 12816

Raymond Thompson Co., 15815 Second Place West, Lynnwood, Washington 98036

Woodstream Corp., Lititz, Pa. 17543

SUPPLIERS

O. L. Butcher Trapping Supplies, Shushan, New York, 12873

Cronk's Outdoor Supplies, Dept. 104, Wiscasset, Maine 04578

E. J. Dailey's Lures and Baits, P.O. Box 38, Union Hill, New York, 14563

Stanley Hawbaker & Sons, Dept. A-35, Fort Loudon, Pennsylvania, 17224

Northwoods Trapline Supplies, Box 25, Thief River Falls, Minnesota 56701

INDEX